Lyrics from an Old Soul
By: Tatiana Whigham

Lyrics from an Old Soul
Copyright © 2016 by **Tatiana Whigham**. All rights reserved.

No part of this publication may be reproduced, stored in a retrieval system or transmitted in any way by any means, electronic, mechanical, photocopy, recording or otherwise, without the prior permission of the author except as provided by USA copyright law.

All characters appearing in this work are fictitious. Any resemblance to real persons, living or dead, is purely coincidental.

The opinions expressed by the author are not necessarily those of Revival Waves of Glory Books & Publishing.

Published by Revival Waves of Glory Books & Publishing
PO Box 596| Litchfield, Illinois 62056 USA
www.revivalwavesofgloryministries.com

Revival Waves of Glory Books & Publishing is committed to excellence in the publishing industry.

Book design Copyright © 2016 by Revival Waves of Glory Books & Publishing. All rights reserved.

Published in the United States of America

Paperback: 978-1534889880

Table of Contents

Dedication 5
Author's Notes 7
The Dream Hanger 9
   Introduction 10
   Chapter 1 12
   Chapter 2 16
   Chapter 3 21
   Chapter 4 26
   Chapter 5 31
   Chapter 6 39
   Chapter 7 47
   Chapter 8 54
Are you who you are because of what you are? Or are you what you are because of who you are? 56
   Introduction 57
   Chapter 1 61
   Chapter 2 67
   Chapter 3 80
   Chapter 4 87
   Chapter 5 92
Runaway Home 95

Chapter 1: March 9, 1953	96
Chapter 2: September 5, 1962	102
Chapter 3: November 19, 1962	111
Chapter 4: May 12, 1963	120
Chapter 5: July 10, 1963	130
Chapter 6	147
Other Books By Tatiana Whigham	148

Dedication

This book is dedicated to my dear brother, Dominique.

'The great thing about dreams is that they become possible each morning that you believe.'

Love you always!

A poem for you

Not every flower is made to stand alone.

Some are made to be kept

In the company of their own fears,

While others are made to be caged like animals

Sitting in the puddles of their own tears.

But either way,

Of the three you must choose.

Because it's impossible to go through life

Without having your petals of trust, peace, and happiness

Be tainted by the morning dew.

We all must have the rocks and coasts of life,

But even in the rain

A flower can still grow in the midst

Of the Sun's blissful eye.

Rain or shine,

Snow or sleet,

You were made to reign as God's child every day of the week.
So it does not matter
The situation in which you currently sit,
Because just like a flower uprooting itself toward the sky,
No man has the power to take away the meaning of your life.
You were made to stand alone and out casted
Only to be feed with a love that's everlasting.
So the next time that you wonder why there are no
Other buds blooming by you,
Just be reminded that God still has more for you to do!

Author's Notes

Greetings to each and everyone of you! Often times as we go through life, we have an idea of Christian living, but not really a zeal for it. In this piece, several of the characters experience situations that compel them to stumble their way back to Christ. With clear depictions of reality, we get a chance to see real people with real issues making the conscious decision to choose Jesus. Through broken homes, bad relationships, and terrible lifestyle choices, each character has to come to grips with the fact that there are some wounds that only God can heal.

The Dream Hanger covers the lives of three young females who each come from very different backgrounds, yet life has ironically brought them to the same place. As each character struggles to pick up the pieces of life, God's purpose and plan for them becomes all the more real. By trashing their plans, they begin to pick up their dreams and live again.

Are you who you are because of what you are? Or are you what you are because of who you are? is a piece that deals with the lives of two young men, each thoroughly a victim of their own society. Growing up in the city streets, they each become products of what they see. Through a few bad decisions and wrong turns, they each find the path that God has for them on a road to discovering the meaning of life, friendship, and forgiveness.

Runaway Home is about the life of a young girl who has the misfortune of witnessing a terrible incident as a child. This incident spiritually scars her, and causes her to have a skewed outlook on life. As time wears on, it's through the aftermath of this very incident that she will find ambition, life, and love, proving yet again that everything can be used for the glory of God. Even with all of her attempts to escape her pain, God brings her back to purpose.

The Dream Hanger

Introduction

March 21, 2007

Dear Diary,

Today's a bad day. Nothing's going right, nor does it feel right. With every smile and sound of chatter, I begin to whimper. Tears roll down my face with no end. Today, my heart aches with no remedy present. Today, I lie at the table, present for the roast of my failures and setbacks. Afterwards, I am bound to drink the cup of shame and devour the desert of helplessness. Where do I go now? Who am I now?

"Thank God, that's over." I reply half-heartedly to myself, as I get up and close my diary before returning it to its rightful place on my nightstand. Today truly was an awful day, but not the worse to come by far. I once was a child full of hopes, dreams, and plans. I had my whole life planned out. I was going to complete my undergrad in Biological Studies at Brunel University in Knoxtown, Mississippi. Then, I was going to go on to Meharry Medical School in Tennessee on my way to becoming a doctor that specializes in pediatrics, Dr. Rayhana Ebburden. It sounds nice, doesn't it? That was the plan. With that, I was going to be the first child of my family to graduate college. I was, but then, life took a turn for the worst, and now I'm here. Back home, living in my parents' house, attending a junior college, when I'm only twenty-seven credits away from a bachelor's degree. I'm twenty-two years old, never been kissed, never knowing the concept of love, but always bound to the idea of obedience (first to God, then to man). God, where did I go wrong? I did everything right, everything that you wanted me to. Being back home in Beachton, Georgia, just wasn't part of *the* plan. No, it wasn't a part of *my* plan. . . .

Now crying uncontrollably, I close my eyes and roll over, anxious to sleep away my frustrations.

Chapter 1

Rayhana

"Today, we're going to watch a documentary on William Faulkner. He was an aspiring author whose writings revolutionized his generation. He. . ." The words of my American Literature professor, Dr. Stroud, are drowned out by the presence of my own thoughts. While he's still talking, I take pleasure in my own writings. Unlike the works of Faulkner, my writings are actually relevant to me in my distress. Excuse me for being honest, but no amount of energy spent on analyzing the works of some early 20th century buff is going to get me out of here. I need a plan; I need an escape from this place, it only serves as a constant reminder of what I've already lost.

The bell rings, and class is over. I have about an hour or two until my next class of crap; so, I think I'll spend it in my own company.

****

Danielle

Who's ever lifted his eyes and really wished upon a star? Was it real or just imaginary? Who's ever closed his eyes to envelope himself into a happy ever after? Yeah, me neither. I used to believe in wishes and happy endings, but now, I know the truth. Dreams and hopes of fairytale living are as close to raw hogwash as anyone can get. The idea of fairness, and you get what you put out is horse crap. Life's not fair, and in the real world, good girls always finish last;

in my life anyways. Here I am, on the cemented steps as they hoist me up to see every detail of my tormented life. There's a liquor store on the corner of East and 1st, a few more apartments just like mine, dusty sidewalks, streets covered with snow, and finally, the empty warehouse at the end of the block. I used to believe that I could leave this place if I tried hard enough, but that's not reality. I've been in this same rut for seventeen years, six months, two weeks, and three days. I'm pretty sure my future is set.

"Danielle, there you are. Girl, I've been looking all over for you." Robin, my best friend for all extensive purposes, who's just another short, plump, brown-eyed girl from the projects with fish lips and high cheekbones. The absolute last person I wanted to run into today.

"You haven't looked far."

"You missed third period! What's up?" Nosy, did I forget to mention that? She's very nosy.

"Staying black and minding my own business."

"It's your junior year. Keep this up and you'll never graduate. And nobody wants a dumb broad."

"It takes one to know one."

"Ha! Ha! I see you got jokes. But for real, I worry about you sometimes. You used to be a fun, nerdy chick that stayed on 'A' honor Roll. Now you act like coming to class is worse than living on death row. To tell you the truth, you haven't been acting like yourself since Randy got…"

"Don't even say it. Don't even speak his name!"

"Since Randy got killed. What happened to him, happened to him. Don't curl up in the grave and die with him!"

That's it. I'm out of here.

"Oh, where are you going?"

"Far away from here. You know I'm so tired of you always bringing this up like it's some kind of trump card. That was my brother. You will never understand."

"Danielle, don't act like he was some war hero who died defending his family's honor. He was a drug-dealer, in the game like everyone else. He knew the life as well as the consequences that came along with it, yet he ignored them and went on about his business."

"He only dealt to bring food into our house! You know what, I'll see you later." Off I go, down the steps and into the streets, yet again.

"Danielle!"

I keep walking.

"Danielle! You can't keep running forever."

"I'm good at it, so why stop now?" I can't believe she went there. Randy wasn't just my brother; he protected me. Without him, who else do I have?

I enter the bar on the inside of the nearby warehouse, a usual spot for me now days.

"Hey, hey."

"Hey, Ms. Lady. You know, it's a little early in the day... Not to mention that it's illegal to sell to minors."

"Yeah, I know. So why don't you just pour me some anyway?" I need something fast, and I'm in no mood for her crap today.

"Alright, but just know that whatever trouble you're trying to chase away will still be there after this drink . . . or two. . . . Seven, or eleven."

"Yeah, whatever." Two shots of gin have become my daily dose. My brother's dead, my mom's always mad at the world, and my father (who by no way deserves the name) left us to move south with his new wife (some foreign chick) and their children. Some life, hmmmm.

Chapter 2

Holiday

March 28, 2007

I fear that the end is near: the end of my world, the end of my dreams, and all that that really means. Maybe I'll become inspired again. Maybe not. I just want for one day to know how it feels to win.

What piece of craziness is this? A little vague for a poem, don't you think? I tell you, working at Shantel's Jazz Spot gets weirder and weirder every day. Tonight, like every Wednesday night, is talent night. We get a lot of singers, painters, comedians, poets, and musicians to showcase their talent. Some of the musicians are so talented; they'll play you right to snooze-blues having you move to a whole different tune, I promise you. Others just better be glad that there aren't any tomatoes in the building.

"Holiday, take care of table seven."

"I got it, Stu. You just worry about you and I'll handle this."

"Yeah, alright."

Stu serves as our local cook, bouncer, and janitor when needed. I sure wish that I had his energy.

"Hey girl, are you alright?" I ask Rayhana as I make my way to the counter to reload my tray. She's a new girl from Mississippi that started about two weeks ago. She goes to school during the day, and works here at night.

Though she never says so, most times she's busy trying to figure out how to get up outta this dump.

"Oh, I'm fine. I just didn't get too much sleep last night. But I'm fine."

"Yeah, whatever. You just better not let Toni catch you like this. You were ten minutes late for your shift yesterday, and fifteen minutes late today."

"I know, I'ma get it together. I promise. I'm just in such a slump right now."

"Yeah, well slump or no slump, every time you walk through those doors, you better have on a jazz smile that says, 'I'm on time for my shift.'"

"Ha, Ha. . . ."

"Well, I'll check back with you later. People are piling up here and there, and by God, I know we don't have enough tables to seat 'em."

"Alright, see ya."

***

Rayhana

Dear Diary,

I feel like I'm tearing myself in two. I go to school during the day, and work all night just so I won't have to go home. I want to move forward, but what could've been and what should've been of my past causes me to regret the present. I'm surrounded by sweaty men who've had way too much to drink, and women who are just as loose as the fannies that they rode in here on. My soul tells me to trust *in God, but my flesh desires to know why and for what purpose. I just don't see why I needed to complete 3 ½ years of college just to work a minimum wage job (something that I could've done straight out of high school). The girl that I once was, full of dreams and hopes, she's long gone now. I don't even know her anymore, but I wish to God that I did. I don't know where I'm headed. I'm blinded by the common picture of emptiness and wasted talent that lies before me. I just heard a man that can play better than Jimmy Hendricks, Louis Armstrong, and Beethoven put together. Yet, that same man's just recovered from five years of endless addiction to heroin. I've heard comedians funnier than Eddie Griffin and Mike Epps times two, stuck in this crap hole with me. I've seen singers with voices of heavenly angels, singing for $25 a night. Decisions, decisions. The process of making much needed decisions escapes me. I feel like I'm in the middle of the sea. I'm not moving forward or backward, to the left or to the right. I'm just stuck in the middle of the sea, unsure of what awaits me, far from anyone's reach of saving me. God, I wish I wasn't so lost in thought. If only clarity were to be mine. Ta-ta for now!*

"Hey, beautiful."

In slides the black knight of my existence. Pooch is a 25 year-old, nice looking, chocolate-peach, Greek god who always seems to give me the chills. I wonder what happened to him. I often wonder if he's like me, a victim of existence. As he sits in one of the empty stools before me, I gather my thoughts and act cool as if I didn't even notice him at all.

"Hey, Pooch. It's Rayhana, by the way. Don't act like you don't know. What'll it be?" I ask, as cool as I can say it.

"Bottle of Heineken, please ma'am . . . and a side tray with your name and number," he replies with a grin. That sly devil, but he won't catch me this time; I'll put Jesus on him.

"Please, in your dreams. You're lucky that I'm still here. My shift is over in twenty minutes, and I'm out of here."

"You mean I won't be seeing you tonight?"

"Ah, let me check . . . NO!"

"Oh, that's cold. That's alright though, I got you..."

"Hey man, let's go," ejects the heroin addicted musician as he walks to the bar. Gee, he's a lot cuter up close, but a devil in the sand I bet. "I'm not trying to be here all night."

"Man, be cool. We have to wait on Al anyway. Why don't you just sit down, enjoy a drink, and chill out."

The man sits down reluctantly, as if it pains him to do so. He's obviously agitated.

"What'll it be?" I ask, as if by habit. His presence annoys me for some reason. I don't know why, but his vibe just rubs me the wrong way.

"Sweet tea will be fine."

"And while you're at it, drive that tea through Long Island if you can, please ma'am."

"No, sweet tea is fine. Just sweet tea!" He says it with such force that even I am taken aback. Our eyes pass a glance for a second or two, nothing romantic, just a space of confusion. Who is this man? And why is he so darn demanding? But, it is my job to give the customer exactly what he wants.

"Sweet tea it is, sir."

"Thanks."

Chapter 3

Danielle

Here I am, babysitting for my neighbor, to make some extra money. School is behind me now; it's a phase that I never want to go through again. Momma doesn't know that I dropped out yet. She has enough to worry about, I guess. So naturally, I leave the house every morning at 7:30 only to travel up two flights of stairs to babysit for Janel. At 3:45 sharp, I drag my butt right back down the steps and go straight to my room (locking the door behind me) just in case momma feels the need to play 'private-I.' I've been doing this for about a month now, and she still hasn't caught on. Some mother I have. . .

Robin kills me. Just because she's been to bible study a time or two, she tried to put the Word on me last night. Talking about some, 'God ain't pleased with you,' and 'He made you to be more than a couch potato.' She better be glad that we were on the phone and not face to face, because I would've really hurt her feelings then. First of all, I don't spend my time on the couch. She's the one who does that. And it's not like I'm sitting home, lazy, not doing anything. I'm working, and considering my history, 'God should be very pleased with that.'

The baby begins to whine.

"Oh, Parker don't cry. Your mom will be back in a little while."

But still, more crying. Ok, sounds like it's time to walk around the room and see if I can put him back to sleep. Parker is about eight months now. He crawls and stands up, but not walking yet.

"Aww. . . Hush now!" As I thrust a bottle into his mouth, he pulls with all the force left in him. As I sit on the couch rocking him back and forth, I wonder where my life is going now. Ma's been talking some mess about not having the patience for me anymore. Who does that? I always thought that patience for your own child was a given. She's sending me to live with my father, James L. Stephens, and his family in order to set me in my place (whatever that means). The same man that after thirteen years of marriage to my mother felt the need to abandon my brother and I for his *boys* (which he had by some woman who can barely speak English, while he was still married to my mother). He claimed that they needed him more. It's funny how they didn't need him until after momma worked two jobs to put him through dental school. He left my mom without a dime. We lost the house and had to move into these sand bag apartments. Randy and I had to transfer to Central High, while he and his family were out there living the good life. He didn't even have the decency to show up to Randy's funeral; oh, he was working (yeah, right). Now, he lives in some upscale neighborhood in Beachton, Georgia. I'm at a loss. I've never even been outside of Boston.

Parker's asleep now, thank God. I gently take his bottle away from him.

***

Holiday

What is love that it should be misunderstood? What is love that it should flourish, only to one day turn into ashes? What is love that I should care to even try: try to hide my sadness, try to hide my disdain, try to hide the fact that I wish that I could do it all over again? If this is love, I want no part. If this is love, I will forever have such hatred in my heart. What is love that I am to remain a caged animal bound in chains? What is love that the freedom of happiness, joy, and peace have somehow escaped me?

   These words so easily flow through my mind as I wait patiently to see the doctor. Over the past few days, I've been vomiting constantly and bedridden for the most part. I think that I might be coming down with something. I try to calm myself. Man, I hate coming to the doctor. They always start off by asking you questions like, "What seems to be the matter today?" or "My, my, how are you feeling today?" And I be like, "Man, you're the doctor. You should be telling me!" They act just like those darn psych's; they get paid all that money just to listen to you talk, and then end up giving you some high priced medicine that you could've gotten over the counter at the dollar store. I tell you, sometimes, I just don't know what this world is coming to. It's foolishness, just plain foolishness.

  "Holiday McDaniel!"

  Darn, just when I was about to bust my way up out of here.

  "Here I am."

  "Right this way ma'am."

Passing dummy number one, off to see dummy number two.

***

Rayhana

Time's passing by so quickly now. I can barely feel a thing. My routine's become pretty consistent: school during the day (Monday-Thursday), working at Shantel's most nights (Wednesday-Saturday), bible study on Tuesday nights, and church early Sunday morning. Through all of this, I never seem to get enough rest though. I sure wish this line would move faster; I hate crowds. Registration here only means that a bunch of students pile into the auditorium waiting to see the advisors lined up in front. Junior college or not, organization is key. They should've figured out another way to do this. All this standing on my feet ain't cutting it. Everybody is standing around chatting and laughing like this is some kind of social hour. Just as I begin to scan the crowd, I spot a familiar face. Way before I can gather who he is, he spots me. And oh Lord, he's heading my way, smiling. Who is this perp?

"Hey, you're the young lady from Shantel's place, right?"

Ok, this is getting freakier by the second. He obviously knows me, but who in the world is he? "It depends on who's asking." I reply.

"I'm Mitch, a friend of Pooch. I played at the spot a few months back."

Oh, now I remember. He's that rude, demanding, past drug addict musician. Oh, I remember him well. He plays pretty good, sometimes too good. His music gives me the chills, like I'd never felt before, and so does his persona. "Oh yeah, I remember."

"Mind if I keep you company?"

"I'm doing just fine by myself, thank you."

"Oh my bad, I just thought that it might make the wait a little easier if you had somebody to talk to."

Now, I've been tolerating this dupe long enough. "Who? You?"

"I don't mean no disrespect, but I've been watching you for the longest, standing here looking like this is the last place you want to be. I just thought that my company could help."

"Highly observant are we?"

"A little, so what's the verdict?"

"I don't even know you."

"Well, now's as good a time as any to start."

No he didn't. Quite the con I must say. I guess talking won't hurt. You can do that with anybody. He better be lucky that he's borderline handsome. "Suit yourself," I smirk.

Chapter 4

Danielle

"Hey Danny! Are these all of your things?"

"Yeah, and it's Danielle to you." As I get off of the Greyhound, I stare into my father's eyes for the first time in three years. Looks like he's put on about twenty pounds, and his hair, though short, has a few traces of gray in it, but something's missing; the more that I stare at the very man that I once worshipped, the more that he begins to look like the scum of the earth. In five seconds of seeing him, I start to feel the pain of these three years all at once.

"Danielle it is. Oh, come this way. I've parked across the lot." I follow as reluctantly as possible. Glasses! That's it. He must've canned them eager to embrace the world of contacts, finally. Upon reaching the car, I exhale. I don't know how much longer I could've walked with him smiling like this is some happy family reunion. I was made to come; this wasn't a choice.

After packing the trunk, we drive off into the scenery of Beachton, Georgia. Some name. To avoid conversation, I turn the radio up and stare out the window. He tries to interject a few comments, but they escape with no reply.

We're a long way from Boston, that's for sure. A long, long way. . . .

***

Holiday

I'm sorry God for disappointing you. I know that you had big plans for me, but for me, this is as good as it gets. No house, no husband, and no white picket fence. I've fallen into a trap of dead dreams and hopes. My life will never be the same, and that's all she wrote.

I'm pregnant. As I stare at the paper in utter shock, it has my name on it, but it can't be me. According to the smudged ink on the paper, *McDaniel, Holiday* is currently ten weeks pregnant and scheduled for a follow-up appointment in a week. How can this be?

As I sit on the couch pondering the news in the isolated comfort of my apartment, the door opens. In walks Cecil, my live-in boyfriend to others, but to me, he's the scum that's bruises me time and again. To me, he's the alcoholic that I wish that I could get away from, but yet, he's still here.

"I didn't hear you knock."

"That's because I didn't. I got a key don't I? That means that I can come in any time I feel like it" In he stumbles, holding a liquor bottle in one hand and swearing at me with the other. I brace myself, because like a mighty wind, I know what's coming. He's now managed to stand in front of me. "What's that?" he asks, pointing to the paper still in my hands.

"Nothing that concerns you."

"Oh yeah?" he says, infuriated. He reaches for the paper, but before he can grab it, I jump off of the couch and run to the bathroom, locking the door behind me. He follows, beating the door like a ferocious lion, yelling and cursing. I know that the door can't hold him for long. Now drunk and high on cocaine, the wooden door between us is no match for him. In my last seconds of peace, I rip up the paper and flush it down the toilet. He may beat me, but he won't take the one thing that belongs to me. Not this time, not again.

The door flies open. . .

***

Rayhana

June 13, 2007

Dear Diary,

Is life really as hopeless as it seems? Yeah, I've registered for class, but my heart feels like it's somewhere else. With all of this chaos and neglect, this world seems so mean, the one that I live in anyway. No one cares. No one loves. No one hopes. No one helps. Everyone is left to fend for themselves. From the youngest to the oldest, this world gives us no choice. We are all placed in this world of hate, hoping, and praying that in the end, everything will turn out okay.

It's another night at Shantel's, yet the people all look the same. Well, not everyone. You see, since registration, I've been kind of talking to Mitch. I know that nothing will come of it, but it just feels so good to vent to someone, anyone. For some reason, I don't feel the need to impress Mitch when I'm with him, so I'm usually completely honest with him. And strangely, he listens. Not like he's some egotistical guy looking to capitalize on every word that I say, but like someone that really . . . well, cares.

In walks Holiday. Gee man, I haven't seen her in a while. "Hey, girl!"

"Oh, hey."

"Looks like you're the one late this time."

"Oh, yeah. Well, I didn't notice." As she speaks, she holds her head down as if preoccupied by some other thoughts.

"Girl, what's wrong with you?"

"Nothing. Why, does something have to be wrong with me?"

"You don't have to get all grouchy with me. I'm talking to you, and it seems like my words are hitting a deaf ear."

"I'm just really not in the mood, Rayhana."

"And since when do you rock shades in a club?"

"It's just . . . Uhhhh, it's just something new. Look, I don't have to go explaining myself to you."

Following an instinct, I quickly remove the shades. Even in the dim light of the bar, I see what looks to be bruises along her left eye and upper cheek bone. Exposed, she runs off. I follow her into the restroom.

"Girl, what is this."

"It's nothing. I just fell."

"On what, the end of someone's fist?"

"Look, Cecil and I were just talking and I…"

"Is he beating on you?"

"No, no. . .It was an accident."

"Accident. Really? Your face looks worse than Flavor Flav and you call that an accident?"

"It's not that bad. Really, it's not."

"Holiday, call the police. Report him."

"No, I can't."

"Oh yes you can."

"I can't."

"Call the po…"

"I'm pregnant, Ray. I'm pregnant." I stop and noticeably watch as she sobs. Filled with the deepest empathy, I move closer to her as she stands in front of the sink. She cries harder. Not knowing what else to say or do, I put my arm around her and ask, "Does he know?"

"No, no he doesn't," she exclaims half-way through her tears.

Chapter 5

Danielle

At times when we least expect God's grace to cover us, it does, so they say. I'm here at the Hoover's Shelter, home to local orphans and battered women. I don't know why James got me into this. I'm not qualified to work with these kind of people. Most times, a person would need a college degree for this kind of work.

"This is the lunchroom. Students have different lunch times according to their classes." The owner, Mrs. Troup, motions to a room of utter filth. There are old, unsteady tables adorned with gum stuck to the surface, a ceiling of the 1920's (ready to cave in at any moment), half working lights (as dim as the night-time sky), and a line of rodents patrolling all corners of the place. What a dump! After eyeing the place a minute or two, we continue on.

"And this is where you'll be. You'll be helping Mrs. Collier with our kindergarteners."

"Hey, I'm Mrs. Collier. I've been expecting you, Ms. Danielle. Come. . . right this way please."

Mrs. Collier is a thin woman with short hair (natural style, God I pray that I never try that!) and huge bug-eyed glasses.

I follow Mrs. Collier around the class and down the hall to the computer lab. After which, I'm told that my first day will be next Tuesday. Gee, I can't wait . . . like a seventeen year old wouldn't have anything else in the world to do.

The agreement is, I go to school during regular hours (due to the fact that I tested out of the 11th grade and will be attending Beachton High School in fall as a 12th grader) and work at the shelter until about 8pm. On weekends, I work at the shelter full-time, from 7:30am-7pm for a measly $5.15 an hour (minimum wage laws don't apply to youths, they say). James says, *'it's only for your character development.'* We both know that's a lie. He only has me working these crazy long hours so that he doesn't have to deal with me. For these few hours without me, he and his picture perfect family can go on as if nothing ever happened. I just serve as a constant reminder of his past.

Let Robin tell it, life's changes are just God's way of redirecting His children. God, if I'm really Your child and You really want what's best for me, why didn't You give me a father who actually cared? Why did You have to give me to someone who only sees me as his disappointment? his mistake?

***

Rayhana

"So tell me, where are we headed?"

"Can't, you'll just have to wait and see," says Mitch as he turns and smiles that sly cracker-jack smile.

He makes me sick. We've been talking for the last couple of months, nothing serious just friend stuff. He's so nice, calm, and chill. Today is our first meeting (I prefer not to use the word date) outside of the city. We've been driving for over thirty minutes and he still hasn't spilled the beans. The suspense is killing me. I hope it's some place nice, real nice. He'd taped a note to my car last night specifically telling me to 'dress to impress' today, so I did. Nothing too sexy or sluttish, God no! Momma would've killed me. I decided to be more nice-casual. After turning my closet upside down, I finally decided on denim jeans with a silver design on the back pockets, a nice peach sleeveless shirt, short, jean jacket, peach accessories, and peach colored wedges. He has no clue that I got everything this morning.

At first, I was kind of scared to hang out with Mitch. To be honest, listening to Pooch talk about his past, I became kind of terrified of him. But now that I know him, he just doesn't seem at all like the guy Pooch described. He's smart (graduated from Georgia Tech majoring in Flight Management), funny, Christian (he even attended church a few Sundays), very mature to be so young (barely 26 years old), and really down to earth. The only thing that puzzles me is how can such a great guy allow himself to be taken on the wrong path? Why would a man with a bachelor's degree from an accredited institute settle for an Vocational Certificate at a junior college? You know up until this day, we've never formally discussed that, but I plan to tonight.

"Here we are."

After carefully scanning the area, I remain in my seat too frozen to move. "What is this?"

"Come on, you'll love it." Mitch has now gotten out and opened my door. Still sitting, I stare at him in shock.

"Are you serious? You made me get dressed for this. It looks like we've pulled up to some old warehouse in the middle of a junkyard."

He laughs, obviously amazed.

In disbelief, I jump out from my seat to further prove my point. "And look, port-a-potties. Mitch, they have port-a-potties on site!"

"Calm down, they're clean. And it's not a junkyard. It's just a vast area of wide open land. Come on, I'll show you around."

"Okay. . . Ok, but if you try anything funny, you will be seeing Jesus a lot sooner than you think. I got mace."

"Ha, ha . . . come on."

"A hee-hee nothing."

Once Mitch unlocks the door, we go in. The building is huge and strangely, rather clean. Nothing and I mean nothing is in here. Hearing the doors close behind us, I immediately get scared. Why in God's name did he bring me here for?

"You like it? It's called a hanger."

"What's there to like?"

"Hee-hee . . . Hangers are buildings used to store planes when they land. When they're in use, up to three planes at a time can fit in here."

"Oh . . . that's nice and all, but I just don't understand why I had to get all dressed up just to come to some old plane storage and…"

"What are you dreaming for Ray?"

"What?"

"What are you dreaming for? Come sit down with me."

I do.

"You see a few years back, I had all of these great accolades and achievements. I graduated high school at the age of sixteen and I graduated from Georgia Tech at the age of twenty. My major was a five-year program, and I finished it in four. I got my first job at the Atlanta Airlines making good money; I flew on average some four, five days a week. I became everything that my father wanted me to be. My dad was pretty strict on us (my brother and I). I never really knew my mom. He pushed us to do things that he himself had never done. Then one day, my dad died of a heart attack. . . My brother couldn't take it, and a few months later, he committed suicide. I had all the credentials in the world, but right then, none of that mattered. I'd lost everything and everyone that I loved in less than a year. They were dead, and you know what, I was dying with them. I was trying to cope with everything when an economic crash hit our company causing over 200 people to lose their jobs. I was one of them. Unable to keep up with bills, I was losing a grip on life, and fast. Now, back home in Beachton, I had to find some way to cope. I began drinking first, then smoking weed, then, looking for something stronger, and then one of my friends introduced me to heroin. Drugs and alcohol stole some of the best years of my life. One night, full to the max of drugs and alcohol, I was sitting in a park right out there by the highway praying to God for help. Before I knew it, I heard a loud sound and watched as a car left the road and began to sink in the river. Without even thinking, I jumped in and helped the driver out. The driver was an elderly man who couldn't swim. Come to find out, the man was a pastor. To this day, he claims that I was some angel that saved him, but in reality, he saved me. He was the answer to my prayer. That same man helped me to get clean. He not only met my physical needs but my spiritual needs as well. Every Wednesday night, I followed him to bible study. Every Thursday night, I followed him to men's ministry. Every Sunday, I followed him to church service. Learning about God's love and forgiveness made me want to *do* better. It made me want to *be* better. I often come to this place. You see, I've realized that the reason my life was in chaos wasn't so much because of the death of my family, but rather the death of my dreams. All my dreams and ambitions died with them. Like this hanger stores planes, I had stored my dreams in the grave, and left them there. So in light of that, I come to this place to remind myself the power of dreaming. So Rayhana, what are you dreaming for today?"

"Nothing. . . I guess. . . I guess I stopped dreaming to, when I left college. I felt as if my dreams and the possibility of them coming true were over. I just couldn't understand why God would allow me to get that close only to be disappointed knowing that I'll never have it. Tuition went up. My mom got sick. And I had to watch as everything that I'd worked so hard for began to fall to pieces one by one. I got two jobs, applied for different grants, put in essays for different scholarships, and still ended up being a house and a home away from reaching my goal. It pisses me off, you know. Did I expect too much? Did I fly too high? And it's crazy because I actually believed that despite everything, that as long as I stayed in Him, God would give me the desires of my heart. I believed it . . . no, I believed *Him*." Now I'm crying hysterically, God I actually believed You and You didn't help me. When I needed You the most, You didn't help me.

"If you believed Him then, keep believing Him now. God loves you too much to give you anything less than the best. God keeps us from dangers both seen and unseen. And He sees way farther than we do. If He doesn't allow you to do something, it's not because your plan is such a bad idea. It's because in comparison to His plan for you, your plan just doesn't measure up."

"Then why would He let me waste over three years of my life for something He was going to stop anyway."

"No time in God is wasted. If He allowed you to stay for that period of time, it was because you needed something that could only be gotten by that experience. Nothing was, nothing ever is a waste. Just because you haven't graduated college yet doesn't mean you won't. It only means that there's a delay. Jeremiah 29:11 tells us that God's plans for our lives are for our good and not to harm us. Just believe in that."

"How can you say that with all that you've been through?"

"Because of God. I loved my family, but God saw that I loved them more than I loved Him. God is a jealous God. He wants no man before Him. I have resolved within myself, that I am exactly *where* God wants me to be. More importantly, I'm exactly *who* God wants me to be, nothing more and nothing less."

Chapter 6

Holiday

Again, I feel like I can't win. One minute I'm up, and Lord, the next minute I'm down. What'll it be? What'll it be? I thought that the victory was already won. I thought that bad luck was over and done. Lord, rain on me, because I'm losing my grip on reality.

It's another day, another dollar. I'm three months pregnant, working in a club six nights a week, and with no clue of what to do next.

"Hurry up, Holiday. There are two more tables waiting on you."

"Going as fast as I can, Stu"

Gosh, he's really becoming a pain in the neck. Gee wheeze, I hope he gets a life, and soon. As for my life, it's been crazy. Cecil continues on in his rages. If I didn't leave, he was either going to kill me or kill the baby which is just as bad. So in the early hours of the morning, I left my own house. Rayhana and her mom agreed to let me stay with them until I get on my feet. I've had to move my shift to hers because Cecil has been stalking me, calling my job, blowing up my phone with all kinds of crazy messages. The guards know not to let him in, so as long as I'm here, I'm safe. . . I think. Rayhana's been talking about some shelter for battered women, but I'm not so sure. It just seems like the first place a crazy man would look.

"Hey girl."

"Hey, Rayhana. How's it going?"

"Good, a normal Wednesday."

"Not too normal; it just happens to be the Wednesday that Mitch is playing."

"Oh, hush."

"Oh, I've been watching you guys; staying on the phone all hours of the night, sending goo-goo texts, and not to mention the frequent visits. It seems to me like somebody's found her Romeo."

"What? No, no, no. Mitch and I are just friends."

"Hmmm, well try telling that to the guy on the right."

"What guy on the right?.. Oh, Pooch?"

"Yeah, Pooch. He's been eyeing you for the past five minutes."

"I don't know why."

"Really?"

***

Danielle

Alone, in this well of life. No love, no cry...No one to wipe the tears from my eyes. I'm in a world where everyone knows what I should do. Everyone, except for me, and through it all, I long to break free. Maybe if I was prettier or smarter, my life wouldn't seem so bad. But for now, I'm stuck here living with my dad.

"OMG, girl you've been in that country old town for over seven months. Tell me you aren't going insane."

"Ha! Ha! In all honesty Robin, it's like a step away from reality. I feel like I'm in a world all by myself sometimes. If all he wanted to do was kill me slowly, he might as well have put the knife in himself."

"Talk to me."

"You know, I went to a ceremony with them the other night, and I didn't even get to sit with them."

"What? Girl, stop."

"Honey, I'm not lying. That poor excuse of a man had me sitting two tables to the back, so that I could watch him and his family from the back of the room, like I was nobody."

"Girl no, child I would've left a long time ago. No he didn't."

"Honey, you haven't heard the worst of it. When he got up to say his speech, he said in his sophisticated voice, *'I wouldn't be here without my family who's here tonight, my two lovely boys and my beautiful wife.'* Girl, I like to have thrown up in my mouth right then and there."

"Nah, he didn't."

"Girl, yeah, I wanted to stand up so bad and say, *'Don't forget that it was my momma who worked two jobs to put you through school, while you were busy creating this family of yours.'* "

"Girl, I don't know what to tell you. So, have you told your mom yet?"

"No, she won't even take my calls."

"So, what are you going to do?"

"Child, get the heck up out of here. And every time that I look at those two bay-bay kids, I get angry all over again."

"Girl, just chill, to everything there's a time and a season. You just do your part and get through school. When your time is up, you get up and go. Let him have his little family, because we serve a God that sits high and looks low. Don't even sweat that."

"Let me guess, that's something new that you heard?"

"Oh, look who's trying to be funny today? While you're laughing, you need to be in somebody's church yourself."

"Child, last I checked there weren't any Methodists churches here. Every church down this way is either Catholic or Baptist. I don't serve any Mary and I'm by no means Baptist-bound."

"Child you're about to be hell-bound if you don't get yourself together. Like I've been telling you, once you get your faith in order, everything else will have no choice but to fall into place."

"I know, and I do try. I try my hardest to stay gone all day and all night just so I won't have to be here. The less I'm here the better."

"Girl, just stay busy and keep yourself occupied. He's going to get his. Don't worry about that petty stuff."

"Yea, we'll girl I have to go. He or one of those rug rats are bound to bust in at any moment."

"Alright, you take it easy girl and stay prayed up. Bye."

"Yeah, I will. Bye."

I wonder how momma is doing. I haven't heard from her since I left. I'm so glad that school has started already. For the first time in a while, it gives me something to look forward to. This summer was a nightmare. Every time we went to shopping centers, only the boys got something. Every time we went out to eat, he only paid for him and his family, like I didn't even exist. If I wanted anything, I had to pay for it with the little money I have from working at the shelter. He doesn't even introduce me to his friends and colleagues as his daughter. I'm just a thorn in his existence. Braxton and Brian are his pride and joy right now. It kills me to see him play and care for them the way that he used to for Randy and I. They've replaced us, and I hate them for it. Romans 12 talks about being kind to your enemy and loving them despite it all, but I guess I'm not there yet.

"Hey Danielle. . . Come play with me."

"Who is it?"

"Brian."

"Go away and leave me alone."

"Please, Braxton won't play with me."

I put my head under the pillow before me, trying my best to ignore him. Receiving silence, Brian decides to come in anyway. Now standing beside my bed, he pats me gently. "Please, can you play with me?" I look up at him; he's almost in tears. "Braxton won't play with me." I so badly want to say no, but I can't bear to see a child cry. He's the youngest, being only three.

"No, I'm not going to play with you . . . But, go get your toys, I'll watch you play in here." He smiles and runs off to retrieve his toys. It doesn't take him long. Somehow, he manages to pull two tubs of toys into the room. He plays so eagerly, identifying each piece for me. As I look at him, my mind goes back to Randy. I wonder if he was still alive, if. . . If someone. . James in particular . . . cared about him the way that he does Brian and Braxton. Randy would probably be off in college somewhere, maybe even with a family of his own.

***

Rayhana

October 23, 2007

Dear Diary,

How sweet it is to smell the honey of life, which cost me such a sacrifice. I'm glad to see all that I've done as the fun in my life continues to spur on. Mitch and I are still talking; this time a little more seriously. I've even introduced him to momma. She knows about his past, and yet, still she likes him. I've also attended Mitch's church some, and I've even met the pastor that helped him get saved. He truly has turned his life around, and by watching him, it has encouraged me. I've switched my major to LPN, and I should be done in no time. I've started a tutoring program for the children of the community at the church.

It's blossomed so much. I just feel this huge sense of peace. I've concluded that even if I never achieve my dreams exactly as planned, God's plans are still so much better and worthwhile. I've decided to bloom where I'm planted.

Sitting in the lobby of Hoover's Shelter, I'm just so happy for Holiday. She's finally decided to seek help from the shelter to aid her in caring for the new baby. She's so strong; a constant inspiration to me. Speak of the devil, here she comes now.

"So, how'd the meeting go?"

"Good. They said that they would help me get assistance once the baby is born such as Medicaid, WIC, and even donated clothes. They also have a program for the women in the shelter to help provide apartments for mothers in need. The apartments are manageable as far as rent too. Just can't have any men stay with you."

"Which, in your case, is a good thing? How's the security?"

"Good. It's a gated complex with guards that patrol the perimeter all night."

"So when can you apply for the program."

"I just did."

"Great, so are there any more obligations that you have to fulfill?"

"No, not at all. I've mentioned events of Cecil stalking the job and your place, so they've offered me a job and place here."

"Are you sure you want to do this?"

"Yeah, I am. You and your mom have been a great help to me, but it's time that I do what I have to do."

"Ok. . . . I'm so proud of you girl." After giving my best friend a hug, I proceed to leave. "Bye and you take care of yourself."

"Will do."

As I walk outside, the sun shines brighter than it ever did. Somehow, I just know that things are going to turn out great. Yeah God, I think it is. . .

Chapter 7

Danielle

No more parties. No more days of skipping school. No more shopping at Boston's mini mall. No more dreaming of things that I could be. No more wasting my life with glee. I've done made something of myself, and I did it with no one else's help. How sweet it is to finally say that I've been doing well, living life my way.

    It's finally summer time, and I'm on my way home, in a few days anyway. With graduation tomorrow night, there's nothing in the world that can bring me down. Mrs. Collier gave me $50 as a graduation gift. Mrs. Troup gave me a fancy cosmetic bag along with $20. James' gift to me was purchasing my airline tickets. Way back when, that would have upset me, but not now. My time here is done, and in five days, he'll never see or hear from me again. It's clear that he wants me gone just as much as I want to leave. I don't care if he rolls over dead, I won't be present. I can't wait to see Robin and momma; they'll be waiting at the airport for me. I can't stand this house, nor anyone in it any longer . . . except for Brian. Braxton is too caught up with his parents treating me like an outsider. That boy gets on my last nerve. James and his wife are out on their date while I'm stuck here keeping these little rascals. They should've been back hours ago, but who am I to say so. The boys just went off to sleep a little over an hour ago, so at least I finally have the place to myself. I don't know how many rounds of Twister and Checkers I could have taken.

    Knock! Knock!

Oh, that must be them. Leave it to me to talk James up.

"Hello ma'am, is this the Stephen's residence."

As I look at the eyes staring at me, I stare back at him wildly. It's a police officer ringing my doorbell and knocking at my door.

"Yes it is."

"My name is Detective Long. May I ask your relationship to Mr. and Mrs. Stephens?"

"I'm Mr. Stephen's daughter."

"Daughter? I wasn't aware that Mr. and Mrs. Stephens had a daughter?"

"They don't. I'm the daughter of his first marriage. And what do you mean by *had*?"

"Well, I'm sorry to inform you, but there's been an accident."

"Accident. . ."

"Yes ma'am. Apparently, Mr. and Mrs. Stephens were on the road when a drunk driver crossed the median and continued into their lane, hitting them head on."

"Accident. . ." I repeat, almost in a whisper.

"Again, I'm sorry to inform you that . . . That. . ."

"That, what?"

"They didn't make it out alive."

I gasp, as if someone has taken the wind out of me. Oh Lord!

"They're dead ma'am."

Oh Lord, hold me Jesus. Unable to restrain myself, I run . . . run to my room as if the pillows awaited my tears. It's all a dream. In the morning, I'm going to wake up and it's going to all be a dream. Nothing ever happened. No one ever died. It was all a dream . . . a dream.

***

Rayhana

May 18, 2008

Dear Diary,

It's been over a year as you can see. And God has sent a little blessing just for me. Amazing though He is, I can't explain, but God has truly brought about a change. I'm dreaming now, yes I am. I'm dreaming of things that neither eyes have seen nor ears have heard. I'm dreaming of things that some would consider to be absurd. I'm dreaming of completing my LPN. I'm dreaming of expanding the tutoring ministry at the church. I'm dreaming of finally putting my faith to work.

It's hard to believe that I'll be done with the LPN program is just two months. Man, I never thought that I would see the day. I'd be a fool to say otherwise. I haven't completely figured my life out yet, but I'm close. I find myself smiling more, talking more, and laughing more like. . . Like I'm actually happy. Just a few months ago, I was torn and damaged because I couldn't afford tuition anymore. I felt like I'd wasted 3 ½ years of my life, and that my chance for happiness was over. But now I've come to realize, that when God closes one door, He opens two others. I was so isolated in my own mind that I never really took the time to enjoy life, my life. But now, I've gained many friendships, a saved relationship, and finally me. I've done so many things that I never would've guessed were possible. So that's it, God helped me to finally discover me, along with everything that I could be.

***

Holiday

I can feel my heart beating fast at just one thought of my past. How could that have happened? Why did I do those things? If only I could believe that they are now just irreversible mishaps. They help me to grow and help me to live, so that I may never repeat these same mistakes again. I rebuke myself. I rebuke my sin. If only I could make amends with those I've hurt. It's a new year. It's a new time. Hopefully, my future will be more divine.

As I rock my baby boy to sleep, I look around at what finally has become of me. Hoover's Shelter helped me to get a low-budget, two bedroom apartment in a gated complex. I don't have very much furniture, only two sofas, a TV, and a kitchen table set, but I thank God for it (all of it was donated by the shelter). I was also able to get a job as a cook in the shelter's cafeteria. I don't make much, but it's enough to live on and I get free childcare during the hours I work. I'm so proud of myself. If only I would've had the strength to do this three years ago when Cecil made me abort my last child. As I look at my baby, Daniel, my mind goes back to the other baby that could have been. Maybe God will forgive me one day. My worst fear is that He already has, because in all actuality, I haven't even forgiven myself, not completely. I keep feeling like I should've done something, anything. But we can't change the past, can we? Daniel has his own room, his own crib, his own dresser, and most importantly, a mom that loves him very much.

I may not have much, but I thank God that I'm finally free of the Cecil shackles. It's taken me six years to get away from him, six years. But, thank God I made it. Thank God I made it. . . .Made it out alive.

***

Danielle

I talk unto myself hoping to discover my desires and wishes, while trying to look unsuspicious. Do I want to go to college? Do I honestly want to be all that I can be? Hello to my future, good-bye to my fantasy. The only thing that I desire is to be. . . .Me!

I'm back in Boston, trying to figure out what to do. With no family to take them in, Brian and Braxton are here too. Everyone's bugging out. Two weeks ago, I had my life figured out. I was going to do two years at Boston State and then transfer to a four-year school. But now, everything's changed. James is dead, and like his usual character, he left two children in the gap to shuffle their way through life. God, I hate him. He always does this to me. Momma won't keep them. And even worse, she said that if I helped them, she wouldn't help me. So here I am, having to choose between fulfilling my life and saving theirs. God, I hate him for leaving me here. I hate him for making me choose. And even worse, I'm running out of time. Momma gave me two weeks to decide if I am going to college or if they are going to an orphanage. God, I'm only eighteen. I'm only eighteen.

To make matters worse, James had been putting the house up as a way to pay for his lavish lifestyle for years. The house that the boys' called home is now property of First National Bank. Typical James, screw everything up and make everyone left behind pick up the pieces. Typical James. . . God, I really wish that he would've survived. That way, I could've killed him myself. And you know in his will, he left everything to his boys' and his wife. He didn't even mention me. He shut me out of his life for years, but I'm the one who has to pull everything together, I always do.

"I'm sick of this place."

I look around to see where the words were coming from, only to see Braxton staring right at me. I've tried to compose myself during the day time and shed my tears at night. Oh God, I've been so caught up in my own thoughts that I didn't even check to see if they were fully asleep.

"I know, but it'll get better. . . .I promise."

"No! I don't want to be here. I hate this place—"

"It'll be ok."

"I hate it and I hate you!" he says, now almost screaming, "I hate it here. I want to go home. I want my mom. I want my dad. I just want to go home." He's now crying inconsolably. Unable to help him, I sit back in my bed, accompanied by my own tears and grief.

"Me too Brax . . . Me too." I continue to listen to his cries as they carry both him and me to sleep.

The next morning, I get up before dawn to write my mom a letter, her last letter for a while. And it reads:

Momma, I love you. But I know what I have to do. I'm not going to college. I figure that colleges these days are too big for a small town girl like me. Don't cry. Don't look for me. I'm alright. I'll be alright. There's just something that I have to do momma. Please forgive me, I never meant to hurt you, but there's just something that I have to do. Something God's been telling me to do all along. I love you, and always will. . . .

Love,

Danielle

I tape it to the door of the refrigerator, grab my bags and the boys' bags, take my life savings along with my graduation money (now $253.78), and leave my mom's house . . . no *my* house. . . .For the last time. By the time momma wakes up and sees the letter, the boys and I will be half way to Beachton on the Greyhound Express. Bye Momma . . . bye momma.

Chapter 8

Danielle

I wonder if I could touch the sea, how would it be? Will it swallow me, harm me, or will it wrap its loving arms around me? I wonder. . .Or will it lead me safe to the harbor? If I could touch the sea, I'd only see a reflection of me. No storm or tide so big will ever distort the image therein. Who I am is already set, but who I will be has yet to be seen. It all depends on where the sea takes me.

It's now August 8th, the first day of school. Thank God. I think the boys need it more than anything, just to see a familiar face, you know. We've been back in Beachton for almost two months now. I felt that the boys needed to be in a familiar place. If there was one good thing that I learned with James, it was that Hoover's Shelter helps single parents, in which case, I now qualify. I told Mrs. Troup my situation and she helped me get an apartment in a low-budget complex, not to mention that I got my old job back. This time as a full-time teacher for the 2nd grade orphans. I haven't completely given up on school tough. I signed up for classes at the local junior college. So, by the grace of God, I finally can have the best of both worlds. I finally realize that God gives and He takes away. He took two men out of my life, my brother (who I loved) and my father (whom I hated), only to give me two more. Braxton and Brian aren't always a joy to be around, but they're my brothers. They're my family, and I wouldn't trade them for the world. I like to think that in a weird way, they were kind of my graduation present from James. He never could or would accept me as his child, but he left me with two of his. You did good James, you did good.

Are you who you are because of what you are?

Or are you what you are because of who you are?

Introduction

Cam

January 10, 2007

I met this girl once; she was almost too good to be true. Reason I say that is because she reminded me of you. She was short, with dark-skin, and feisty with a smart little mouth. Her accent was country, like she was raised in the south. The words she spoke, she spoke from the heart. I knew right then that this could be my new start. She was a familiar stranger, a lost angel that's been found. I felt tied to her somehow, like our love was on sacred ground. I awoke from this dream, startled, because she was gone and I missed her. It only took a second though for me to realize that the girl that I met was you. . . .

And these are the words of a lonely sucker. Man, I've been calling Brandy all day, and no answer. I'm about to cut her loose for real though if she keeps playing. She doesn't know me, I'm Cameron Johnson, the original 'Cam,' and I refuse to be played like some simp. I crash on my bed, dead beat tired from today's practice. As I kick my shoes off, they fall freely to the floor.

If I had to do one more suicide on that white man's court, today was going to be my last day. All cause Donnie's lame behind air-balled all his free throws, and I mean EVERY last one of 'em. Shoot, if I was that bad, I wouldn't even waste my time dressing out.

With school all day, work in a few hours . . . man, I need a vacation for real. I'm working harder than a Hebrew slave and I ain't but seventeen.

Knock! Knock!

"Who is it?"

"Boy, you better open this door. Talking about some 'who is it'; shoot, the same one who pay these bills."

Man, dang, can't a man get two seconds in peace. Momma is always bugging. "Here I come," I answer, reluctantly unlocking the door. I know I can't say much to her 'cause she's my momma and all, but the expression on my face is a different story.

"Ma'am?"

"Boy, don't ma'am me like you don't know. I need you to watch Lamar tonight."

"But ma how? You know I got to go to work at 7pm."

"And what's that supposed to mean?"

"Ma, I've been at school all day, then practice. I at least want to get some sleep if I can. You know I have to pull an eight hour shift tonight."

"Boy, does it look like I care? Nat's here and I got to go. Here, get this baby," She says, shoving the baby my way.

Poor dude, it isn't his fault. He's only ten months old.

"Talking about you got to work, please what you think I've been doing for the last twelve hours?" Walking to the door in her tank top, jeans, and Chaka-Khan heels, she looks every bit of dead weight. Pulling on that darn cigarette like it's her last breath. Shoot I hope she chokes off of it. "Look, I'll be back when I'm back."

"So what am I supposed to do with him?"

"What you do best; watch his little tail 'til I get back."

And with that, she was off; slamming the door so hard that Lamar busts out screaming just from shock. Lord, I can't take much more of this. My eyes glance at the notebook sitting next to me with a quote that Pastor Roberts said last Thursday at chapel. It came from Romans 8:18, "For the sufferings of this present are not worthy to be compared with the glory that shall be revealed." Shoot, I can't tell it. I mean I'm tired. I have to be to work in less than two hours, I can't get any sleep, I'm hungry, and to top it off, this darn baby's hollering at the top of his lungs.

"Man I hate her!" With tears rolling down my face and me getting madder by the second, I quickly push a bottle into his mouth to shut him up. How does she think this makes me feel? People are always laughing because she's over forty, still climbing in and out of men's beds, and got me at home all the time raising her child. You know, I used to envy kids with active fathers in their life. It made me fantasize about how different my life would be if I had had a father that would come home every day, work, take care of his kids, and provide for his family. Glancing at the frame hanging up on the wall, the only Christian thing that momma has in the house, which reads, 'The God of Zion is just and able to supply all of your needs.' Well if that's the case, God has a lot of explaining to do.

Lost in thought, I glance at Lamar who's now inching his way to sleep. . . .'Bout time. Just to think of it, that's probably what got Brandy acting all funny. Just the other night she tells me that I have MY priorities 'mixed up' and I need to start 're-evaluating' my life. I don't know where she's been, but this is my life. I'm just trying to focus all of my energy on getting out of here. Shoot, with a car and a house, I can leave here and never look back. Just watch . . . one day. . . .One day . . . soon!

Chapter 1

Cam

Walking in the streets with time to beat, makes me feel the agony of my cold, wet feet. With warn out soles and no money to buy something new, I'm about to make life do what it do.

Knock! Knock!

"Who is it?"

"Yo, Sondra it's me!" She opens the door like she's about to knock somebody out.

"Boy, what do you want?"

"I need a favor!" I exclaim, holding my brother up, hoping to get her empathy.

"Cam, now you know I can't watch him tonight. I have to study for my Lit test tomorrow, and speaking of which, you do too. You know it's 25% of our grade."

"I'm not trying to hear that. Listen, I'm heading to work, but I have to find something to do with him first."

"Cam, no. Nope, that not's going to happen."

"Please, pretty please."

"Nope."

"Now you know I'm going to give you a few dollars when I get off."

"You already owe me a fortune."

"Aye, I got my check right here. We can cash it at Yang's store on the corner right now. You'll have your money, and I'll be on my way to work. It's a win-win. To make it even sweeter, you can be standing right there when I cash it to make sure that you get your money off top."

"Ok, but let me ask momma to watch Lamar until I get back."

I hand her the baby, who's now fast asleep, along with his bags.

"I'll be right back."

Thank you Lord. With that out of the way, all I have to do is cash this check and work my eight hours tonight in peace. Let's see, I'll get off at five tomorrow morning, sleep through first period (shoot, I'm already failing), go to the gym and study for Lit through 2nd block and lunch, then take the test, and cruise for the rest of the day. I'm off Wednesday and Thursday, which is a first, and I'm going to enjoy it to the fullest.

"Alright, let's go," says Sondra, now fully dressed for the weather. Sondra was a cool girl. Being my neighbor since I was like twelve, she's obviously the best friend that I have, and the most annoying. She is medium height, brown-skinned, with a head full of oversized braids. I don't know why she wears weave anyway, her hair's already past her shoulders.

"You call that getting ready. What are you the Eskimo of Baltimore?" We both laugh as we go down the steps.

"Keep laughing. It's cold out there."

"It outta be. It's the middle of January. A little frost won't hurt anybody."

"A little? Last time I checked, that 'little' frost was all over the city streets."

"With weather like this, you'd think that they'd cancel school."

"For what, so low-lifes like you can have a legitimate reason to skip."

"Ha! Ha! I see you got jokes. But watch, in about five years, I'm going to blow-up. I can hear the fans screaming my name right now, 'Cam! Cam!'."

"Really, with what? I hope you're not talking about those skimps you call rap."

"Please, if I don't go big in the NBA, I'm going to be like one of the greatest sports' commentators of all time. I'm going to be legendary."

"Says who?"

"Your momma, the last time I checked." I run down the lobby hall trying my best to dodge the blow that I knew was coming.

"Ooooooh, I'ma get you."

"You have to catch me first."

Out the door we go, running and playing into the streets. We were just kids. We had no idea the type of trouble that we would meet.

***

Zay

"Put the money in the bag." I stare at the cashier, who's obviously too distraught to move without crying like a fool.

"Hurry up!"

"Yo Zay, we ain't got much time. Just get it and go."

"Man, don't say my name," I yell, with my pistol still raised at the cashier. "Just get the tape and bust out."

"Please, please don't hurt me," mumbles the cashier in between sobs as she slides what appears to be seventy-eight dollars across the counter. I re-count it just to be sure.

"What? Seventy-eight dollars. Yo, you better bend down under that counter and pull some more money out of that safe."

"I don't. . . .I don't have anymore. Please, don't hurt me."

Realizing that I'm getting nowhere with this chic, and with time ticking faster by the second, I jump across the counter and investigate the safe myself. And sure enough, the safe was empty. I guess it's safe to say that Yang, her father who's just as prejudice as he can be, didn't even trust her with the money. Out of options and with no thoughts of what to do next, I get up from the counter just as quickly as I know how.

"Yo man, you got the paper?" yelps Kenny emerging from the back, with the surveillance tape in hand.

"What paper? They don't have any money. Nothing but seventy-eight dollars." I hold the money up in the air for him to see, while still holding my pistol in the direction of the cashier.

"What about the safe?"

"Nothing."

Thoroughly as shocked as I am, Kenny did the unthinkable. He raises his 9mm and shoots the cashier dead on the spot. Shocked and confused, I watch aimlessly as the blood runs from underneath the victim. From what I can see, she is already gone.

"What did you do that for? She was telling the truth."

"You knew that it was going to happen sooner or later. Why are you tripping?"

"It wasn't like she was grown. She couldn't have been no more than sixteen."

"Well, next time they'll know to stack the register with some real change."

I look back at the young girl and her lifeless body. This is really the first time that I have ever been around a dead person before and to think that the bullet that killed her came from my own brother. I bend down to cover her wounds, and check her pulse; one that I knew was already gone. With no thoughts of what to do next, I start performing CPR as best I know how.

"Get up Zay. We have to go," yells Kenny, uplifting me up from the nameless face that stared back at me. And it was bad timing too. Just as we were about to exit, in walks two teens giggling and smiling. Boy, did they pick the wrong time.

The boy notices us first, stopping dead in his tracks. Kenny, who seems to process the situation a lot faster than I, raises his 9mm as if daring the two teens to move. Seconds go by, as each person tries to figure out the best move. The girl, who obviously recognizes the victim, (which is in clear-view of where she's standing) let's out a scream and moves toward the counter that's guarding her fallen friend as the boy moves in the opposite direction. Not thinking, just going off of reflex, I guess, Kenny shoots her. But just before he can shoot the boy, he makes a leap to the left, having the snack chips cover him from the bullets coming his way.

"Kenny, let's go! Come on brah, let's bounce."

And with that, Kenny and I leave the store, jump into the car, and head back to Springfield, just a few miles away. Not even looking back, not even trying to remember. . .just riding.

Chapter 2

Cam

February 13, 2008

    Deep in the heart of North Branch Correctional Institute, I'm writing to you to see what it do. With dreary smells and dim lights, Lord how in the world did this happen at the peak of my life. I was on the rise, five more months to finishing my senior year, now I'm sitting in a cell for what the Judge says is 15-10. A max of fifteen years for a crime that I didn't commit, but all they saw was a black kid who's family struggles to pay the rent. A black kid, slumping in the city's streets, could not be trusted in their eyes to tell the truth every day of the week. Sondra's gone, dead on site, so excuse me for saying so, but now, I don't really care what happens to my life. I was seventeen years old at the time, so they tried me as an adult, now the prison cell is my life and that's all she wrote. Who am I, and why am I here, is all that I'll have to ponder for the next few years.

    I close my notebook, now my only companion. Sondra's gone and so is Ellease. She was working at the shop that night until her dad came back from depositing that week's earnings. Yeah, she was kind and she was sweet, but now, she's just a memory lost and gone. I explained to everyone what I saw, but the Prosecution chopped that up to a delusional teen talking his way out of guilt. With no one on my side, not even my own momma (who sold me out like some two-bit thief) telling people that I can't be trusted and had a history of stealing. I've never been in trouble in my life, and the time that I did get something out of her purse, I was only trying to get the money back that she stole from me. I couldn't afford an attorney, so they assigned me some dumb court appointed defense attorney, who probably believed that I was guilty anyway. I was facing two counts of 1st degree murder. With no options, and all of the odds against me, I took the plea bargain for two counts of manslaughter. I was going to rot anyway, might as well choose the one that gives me a chance to see daylight.

Lying back on my bed, staring at the ceiling above, it just doesn't seem like there's any justice nor is there any voice for the right. I've lost everything important in my life. My brother's going to grow up on his own for all that I know. Brandy won't even return my letters. And I haven't seen momma since the day I stepped in here, and that's been about thirteen months now.

I think about Sondra every day. Sondra's momma sent me an obituary and some pictures of her. I guess she's the only one in the world who believes me. I taped them to my wall to be sure that I'll never forget her. My biggest fear is forgetting her voice or even her smile. Man, they wouldn't even let me go to the funeral. I keep replaying that night over and over again in my head. Trying to figure out if there was anything that I could've done differently to change what happened, but I can't think of anything, anything that matters.

"That's your girl?"

I turn around to find the voice that interrupted my train of thought; only to find that it's Mc'Run, my new roommate for all extensive purposes. He must've caught me glancing at the pictures on the wall, lost in the moment.

Not deserving of a reply, I just give him the stare, one that reads 'Leave me alone.'

"She's cute," says Mc'Run, half-eyeing me from the pages of the book that he's reading. Still silent, I had to agree with him. She was beautiful inside and out.

"So what happened?" he asks flipping the pages through his book.

This fool is questioning me like this is some kind of social hour or something. If I wanted to talk, I would've said something by now. All he does is sit around here and interrogate people. Dude has to be over sixty, sitting up here like some king pin with them Malcolm X glasses on. And those high water blue and white strips aren't doing him any justice.

"What happened? She got tired of waiting on some punk like you to get your act together?"

That's it; he just struck a nerve. I get up from my cot to confront the man in front of me. "Worry about yourself old man and let me do me."

"Ooooooh, so you're a man now?" he chimes as sarcastically as ever while still reading his book.

I really don't want to fight today. This is my third prison in a little over twelve months and my 5th roommate in the clan. I really don't want to shank this old man, but he's pushing it right now.

"Something like that."

"What did she do? Send you a Dear John? Tell you how you don't you fit in her life right now —"

In the middle of his sentence, I jump on that fool. After the first few seconds, it's evident that this man is a lot stronger than he looks. In three maneuvers, he had\s my tail face down on the floor.

"I wouldn't try that again if I was young blood," he demands, half-throwing me across the room, only to return to his chair to flip yet another page of his book.

Not willing to go down as a simp, I realize right then and there that my next attack would have to be well-thought out.

"So, you were saying?"

"What happens in my life doesn't have anything to do with you."

"So she did leave you."

"She's not your concern."

"Nope, obviously she's yours," he replies, now looking up at me from the pages that flustered in his hand. "What's your name young blood?"

"They call me C-low," which was a name that I had acquired in prison, and to be honest over the last few months, I had actually begun to take a liking to it. It made me sound fierce, dangerous, and completely lawless.

"I meant your government name. None of that street crap you and the other little rascals are into now days."

"Cameron. Cameron Johnson."

"I'm Manfred Cen-Clair Rundwarf III, but everybody calls me Mc'Run. What are you in for? Robbery? Grand theft? Not paying your lunch money on time?" He jokes, closing his book as if to get into some serious conversation.

Feeling annoyed, I manage to get a response out before heading back to my bunk. "I'm here for murder. Two counts."

"Oh, murder! Did you do it?"

"That's why I'm here, isn't it?"

"There are always three sides to a story: your side, their side, and the truth. I'm asking you for the truth. Did you do it?"

Feeling as if someone is actually hearing me, my words begin to roll off of my tongue faster than water.

"No . . . No I didn't."

And there it was just like that, I found myself for the first time unfolding myself to some two-bid stranger that I'd only met sixteen hours ago. But he's different, unlike everyone else over the last few months, he actually listens.

***

Zay

February 21, 2008

Riding and clowning, doing dumb stuff became the usual for me and the family. No momma, no daddy, all I have is Kenny. But man, I wish to God that I didn't. Man ole' dude is reckless, with no limits on life. I tried to break away time and again, but gang life ain't a place where you jump out and jump in.

Passing by the school every day, I see this sign that reads "If you're lost, Jesus is the way." But if Jesus is so big, why can't He get me out of here. I'm trying my best to uproot myself, but I'm running out of options. On one hand, I'm trying to go to college and better myself, but on the other hand, shoot I'm depending on blood-money to pay tuition. And it's so crazy because when I was younger, I often wondered what it'd be like to have that one homie, that one life-long friend that was on the same path that I was on. You know what I got . . . . My brother Kenny. If that was my answered prayer, go figure.

"Yo, Zay there you go. I've been looking for you."

I look up to see Kenny walking into my room as if there's no door at all. I really hope that someday he learns how to correctly use a closed door, 'knock and it shall be opened.'

"Well, I know that you haven't looked far."

"I'm saying though. Your phone's going straight to voicemail. Cal and Dee said that they haven't seen you at the spot in a couple of days. What's up?"

"I've been hitting these books, trying to be an Einstein."

"Shoot, a black one." Both of us bust out laughing, just like we used too.

"But 'aye, that's cool and all, but tonight, I'm going to need you to come through. I got two hot rides and both of them need to hit the chop shop. I already got two buyers ready to put down some serious paper if you know what I mean."

"Man, can't you get Tom, Cal, or even Sed to run that. I got two tests tomorrow."

"Man come on Zay, I see you trying to be all philosophical and what not. But we both know that people coming out of junior college don't make any money. I'm trying to help you make some serious paper, and I'm talking about money. Are you in or are you not?"

Feeling that to be more of an ultimatum rather than a question, I half heartedly agree.

So that's that, we leave the house and hit the road like always. Another day, another dollar. Stopping by the South side, we pick up Cal and Dee crazy selves. Looking around the car, I see that everybody's smiling, but no one is thinking, not past the moment anyway.

"So Zay, I heard about your stand up." peeps Sed's coward-behind as he muffles his way into my thoughts.

"Oh, yeah," I reply, not really wanting to discuss the situation.

That happened months ago, and really all I want is to continue living my life as if it hadn't. 'Cause to be honest, Kenny's been cursing the path of no return ever since. It's like he threw away the rule book, 'how to keep your life 101.'

"Man, I heard ya'll took two down and robbed it. I bet that non-English speaking Yang will think twice next time before he calls somebody else a nigga."

Everyone in the car burst out laughing as if one man's actions justifies the death of two people. That sickens me, but I smile because for all I know, brother or not, my life may depend on it.

"Man please, I did that. This chump was so amp to go in there and rob it, but froze like a Popsicle when we got there. Like a statue or something man," jokes Kenny, mocking me as best he can. He loves to take credit for the most treacherous things, but he can have it. I don't want my name nowhere near anything of that nature.

As everyone else makes their own private joke, I turn my head to the window and participate in my own private thoughts. A couple of days before we robbed Yang's store, I was going through the initiation process of the gang, the Serious 7's. I had to do one of the three: kill a nigga, rob something, or beat up someone beyond recognition. I'm not a fighter, and I definitely wasn't about to kill nobody. So I went around looking for places to jack, easy money you know. The night before, we stopped by the store to get some drinks. But the owner was so rude and condescending (following us around the store, talking smack like just because we were black, we didn't have money or couldn't afford anything). That night he gave us the perfect reason to jack him. But now, I almost feel sorry for the ole' dude. He lost his money and his daughter. Turns out she was in high school; she would've graduated that May, but . . . . she had to meet Kenny. . .no, she had to meet *us*.

Cruising the streets and coming to a stop, we edge our way into Parker Hills, which in our community is an absolute no-no. Parker Hills is the place where all of the doctors, lawyers, and well-to-do people live and shop. This is not an area to rob; this is an area to get killed in. Judging from the silence in the car, I'm not the only one who sees this as a death trap.

"Man, Kenny what are you doing?" asks Cal, the only one in the vehicle who has the courage to speak.

"Working! I'm tired of always copping the hood. We need to expand our market. Man, we need to get better material. What better place than here?" chimes Kenny as his smile stretches from ear to ear.

"But you told me that you already had two cars lined up." I say.

Pulling into the shopping plaza, he replies, "We do . . . Man just look around, any two in this parking lot will do." He parks the car amongst the well-off, a place where we know we don't belong. "But first, I need to make a withdrawal." He pulls his 9mm (which he's been doing all the time, usually for no reason at all, since the robbery) from underneath the seat, and gets out of the car and everyone follows him but me.

"Zay, you coming?" he quips.

"Nah man, you got it."

"Well, make yourself useful and watch the car." Watching them go in and not really knowing what to do, I move over into the driver seat.

Kenny is bugging out, and I mean bad. Nothing's good enough. It's almost like it's a game to him or something. Shoot, with time ticking and nobody in sight, I'm getting more impatient by the minute. I mean anything could be going wrong right now, and sadly, there's nothing that I could do.

Knock! Knock!

Startled and confused, I turn to the window and see the person on the opposite side. He motions for me to let the window down and I do.

"Problem officer?"

"No, not yet. I'm just patrolling the area. You lost?"

"I'm just waiting on a friend, that's all."

"Well, you try your best to stay out of trouble. You hear?"

"Yes sir!"

At almost the exact moment, out comes Kenny and the crew. Apparently as shocked as I am, they freeze dead in their tracks. Think fast Kenny, just like you always do.

As the officer turns to leave, he comes face to face with what has to be his greatest fear. When he turns to look back at me, it's like his eyes are trying to figure out whose side I'm on. Kenny, obviously taking advantage of the situation pulls out his 9mm, and raises it toward the officer. Not really knowing what to do, I jump out of the car to block what I knew was coming.

Bang! Bang! Bang!

As we hit the ground, I check myself for injuries, and sure enough, I got hit in the thigh. I turn toward Kenny, who's shaking his head at me in betrayal.

"Come on Kenny. We have to go. Let's book," yelps Sed, who's already long gone in the distance. Kenny follows in fear rather than purpose.

I roll back over in pain, facing the officer who I tried my best to save. "You ok sir?" With one look, I know that he isn't. "Sir, Sir... Get up sir! Get up!" I push and shake him but to no avail. He's dead, and my hands are covered in his blood.

Seeing people come out screaming and yelling, I know my chances are slim. So with one last glance at the fallen officer, I make my way to the car which proves to be more difficult than before. I start her up, and ditch town. With so many thoughts, I just drive. I can't go home, because my brother and his crew will be there (and by the look on his face, I know that I'll be marked). And I definitely can't go back to Parker Hills, because who would believe a black kid in the presence of a dead cop. Out of options, I just drive. Running red lights, hitting curbs, I just go. Hearing sirens behind me, I push the gas even harder, down an alley, across one intersection, and then I hit the bypass. Now with three cars tailing me, I take the nearest exit, Exit 121 down to Central Lane. I make that left and hit opposing traffic. Driving recklessly, against the odds, I press on anyway. Making it back to the main streets, I then cruise down alleys and back roads. I come down one street with three to four cars behind me, and then one car jets out in front of me as if to block my path. With my adrenaline at an all-time high, I quickly make a right taking me back into the city.

With one quick move from the car on my left, he bumps me into the lane of opposing traffic. I swerve to miss an oncoming vehicle and lose control. Flipping and turning along the icy streets, I slam into somebody's oak tree. Having no seatbelt on at the time, I'm thrown a few feet from the vehicle itself. With virtually no energy to move, I roll over looking to the sky for help. But all I see are officers with their weapons raised, a few are yelling and one officer is reading me my rights. I'm thrown into a police car, handcuffed and all. Lord I guess it's true, 'great men really do have a great fall.'

***

Zay

November 23, 2008

With robbery, murder, and resisting arrest on my rap sheet, my life's no longer bitter sweet. Dreams of college and even a future can no longer be my home, because with a fifty-five years to life sentence, North Branch Correctional Institute is now the place where I must rot alone. Zaycon Robinson, so they say, is now entering prison, so make way.

Word has gotten out on the streets of how I betrayed the set, so I've had gang members routinely trying to make me pay some unforeseen debt. But I'm holding my own, as best I can. Man prison ain't no place to raise a man. There's fighting, drugs, and drama; all the while I'm still trying to wrap my mind around it all. In just nine months, I've been in the hole three times, but I'm not complaining, population sucks. A new roommate, a new cell. With every fading day, I feel like I'm rotting in hell. I haven't heard from Kenny since I got here, but according to Dee, he's still out there acting a fool. It should be him in here instead of me. The way I see it, I'm just a victim of the society that surrounded me, but none of that matters now.

Chapter 3

"Come on Mc'Run. You're going to make us late."

Usually, I'm not the one to rush to the cafeteria, but its Thanksgiving, one of the few days out the year when the food is somewhat good. I can taste the ham-hocks now. With cornbread, white rice, and mustard greens, man I'm about to dig in for real.

"Cam, I don't know what you're rushing for. We still have to wait 'til roll call."

"Yeah, yeah."

In about five minutes, roll call began. Adjusting to prison life isn't an easy thing, but it's doable. I'm just glad that the Lord saw fit to give me a roommate like Mc'Run. Being of age, he became the father that I never had. Instead of fighting, fussing, and making a fool of myself, he taught me that in order to make something of my life, I had to become a great thinker. Reading about people such as Micaville and Nelson Mandela makes me think that I might have a future after all. With his help, I even got my GED. Being a man of his stature, sentenced to seventy-five years for a rape and murder that he didn't commit, he's always so positive and Christian too. He has this saying though that, 'God does everything for a season and a reason.' I wish I knew why He put me here, what good can I do behind cell walls?

Walking into the chow hall and getting my plate, it seems that I see a familiar face. Ole' dude's maybe 5'8 or 5'9, but I can't think for the life of me where I know him from. Judging from his looks, he's not a ball player. And I know for sure that he didn't go to Jackson High.

"Well, are you going to stare or are you going to eat?" says Mc'Run as he interrupts my thoughts.

"Oh yeah, my bad." As I go on stacking my plate a mile high with yams, and mashed potatoes and gravy, it hits me. I was so busy traveling memory lane that I forgot to get my slice of cornbread. As custom, I would have to start all the way at the end.

"Man!"

"What's up?"

"I forgot my cornbread."

"Cam, don't tell me that you're going all the way to the back of the line for a piece of bread."

"Well, are you going to give me yours?"

"No! Man it's Thanksgiving, I'm not giving up my bread for nobody."

I had two choices: to go to the table without cornbread or to endure another five to ten minute wait in line. Looking at my plate, it's obvious.

"I'll meet you at the table then."

And off I go down the line. As I settle into my position, Ole' dude is like three or four spots in front of me. He looks so familiar, but I just can't place him. But prison is not a place where you stop and stare. So, I glance from time to time, but never long enough to cause any interference. He looks to be a few years older than me, maybe twenty to twenty-five. But age is nothing but a number in here. You live by the set, and you die by it. And judging by the looks of things, he had to be part of the Serious 7's (because from where I stand, I can clearly see the seven lines tattooed above his left wrist). They were known to be ruthless in these parts, not caring about anybody. Gang life maybe for some, but it's just not for me. As we move up in line, I finally hear his voice, and then it hits me.

***

Zay

"Man you're stupid."

I listening to my roommate, Ron, go on and on about the food during the holiday season in here. I've never been in here for the holidays, but Ron, he's been in here just about eight years now so he would know.

"Zay, man I'm serious. Usually, the food ain't all that hot, but on holidays. Man, they go to work. With sweet-water cornbread, white and yellow rice, all kinds of meat, greens…"

"Man, I won't be eating it."

"Shoot, then slide it my way."

Both of us burst out laughing not really aware of what was coming next. Within a few seconds, I am on the ground from a blow so hard that I wasn't sure where I was. As I roll over to defend myself, all I see is some little cat swinging blows like he's running with the wind. Being a little stronger than him, I manage to overpower him and get back on my feet, but this little cat is relentless. With two blows to the head, he comes back and catches me with a jab. If you're in the Serious 7 set, man you can't be going places getting beat down, especially not by some little nigga. So I have to protect my reputation.

After only a few minutes (which seem like hours), a few officers jump on the scene separating the two of us. In most cases, the officers wait and apprehend the loser. But in our case, I guess they got tired of watching, so we both went down. All the while, I can hear that little cat screaming from the top of his lungs, "Nigga, you dead!" as he's carried off into the distance. Into the hole we go.

***

Cam

March 7, 2009

Revenge is a dish best served cold, though often bitter sweet with lasting memories forever present to unfold. I saw him, but he didn't see me; the one he left sentenced to a lifetime of grief. Never would I have thought to see him again, the words I'd say or the fight that I'd be in. Nonetheless, it makes no difference now, nothing I do can turn back the hands of time, but the thought of paying him back the sufferings of mine will somehow give me peace of mind.

"Jesus, Cam, I thought that you'd out grown all that foolishness. How many times do I have to tell you, the fist is a poor man's excuse?"

Turning to Mc'Run, I close my journal, readying myself for a long conversation.

As his words fade beneath my own thoughts and feelings, I've had four months of nothing but time to reflect on things. I often wondered what the guy thought. Did he even recognize me? Apparently not. I've been advised by my counselor, Mrs. Fisher, to enroll myself into a Tier program, because (and I quote) 'the Serious 7's got a hit out' on me. I know that anytime you beef with someone in a gang, the set steps in to defend them. But man, they can come on; I don't have anything to lose.

"Cam, are you even listening to me?"

Turning back to Mc'Run, I sit up ready to prepare my reply.

"It's him."

"Him who?"

"It's one of the guys who killed Sondra. It's him."

Stunned and shocked, Mc'Run paces the floor momentarily, and then takes a seat next to his bed. "I know what you must be feeling right now, but if God brought you to it, trust and believe that He will bring you through it. I can't sit here and tell you what all I'd do if I had the chance to right my wrongs, but son, you're going to need God to help you through this one. And if you don't think so, then you're a darn fool. If you ain't never needed Him before, you need Him now." He takes a moment of silence, allowing his words to sink in all the more. "You see, when someone takes something from you, a part of you goes with 'em. But if you don't fight for anything else, son you need to fight for your right to live . . . again."

As the tears roll down my face, I know that he's right. But sometimes, doing the right thing seems like the hardest thing to do. . .

***

Zay

Life in prison is far from a dream, but this just happens to be the life that God has chosen for me. No, it ain't pretty nor is it filled with bells in the air, but it's the one place that harbors both pain and regret enough for everyone to share. Everyone's fighting a battle to others unknown that causes them to go through life forever alone.

After the fight episode, it's is Counselor Fisher's brilliant idea to have the two of us detail together: first the chapel, then the yard, and now it's the laundry room. I'll tell you one thing; this cat sure doesn't talk much. According to roll call and count time, his name is Johnson. From the look of things, he's not a part of any gang. Word in the cell is that he's a loner it's just him and his roommate all day, every day.

Folding clothes, washing clothes, drying clothes, and ironing clothes, I promise you spending sixteen hours a day in this joint will make anyone go insane.

"You talk?" I ask, trying to make conversation, but to no avail. It's already been two hours, I'm not about to spend the next fourteen hours speechless. Whatever beef this cat's got with me will have to be settled right here and right now. "What? Cat got your tongue or something?"

Thoroughly ignoring me, Johnson continues to iron the clothes in his bin.

His calmness makes my temper boil. All that talk, fighting and what-not, and when we get face-to-face the nigga's speechless. Refusing to be ignored any longer, I quickly ball up a couple pieces of clothes in my bin and aim straight for his head. Boom (a direct hit)! "You got something to say now?"

Within seconds, it's the fight of a lifetime. A jab here, a cross-body hit there, and so on. The only difference this time is that there are no officers to stop it. As the moments pass (seeming to be like hours), bins are overturned, clothes are scattered, and washing powder is spread everywhere. Tired and exhausted, we're just hanging on each other and swinging, each not willing to give up the fight.

"Man, I'm tired of you."

"I'm tired of you; you and your brother."

"My brother?"

"Yeah, I've been waiting to see ya'll again."

"Nigga, I don't even know you."

"You sure about that? Take a real good look."

I back up into a corner, trying to place the young man standing before me, but nothing, and I mean nothing comes to mind.

"Oh what, you don't remember? The store? The robbery? The girls? It's your fault that I'm even in here."

After only a few seconds, I finally realize who this boy is. He's the same guy that Kenny tried to shot the night of the robbery. Here he is, alive and in the flesh. Unable to stand, my legs collapse beneath me, and I make my seat on the floor along the wall.

Chapter 4

Cam

April 16, 2009

Usually, Mc'Run and I head to the library for a little bit after breakfast, but he decides to go to the clinic today. Turns out he came down with a cold or something a few days ago. And you know that it has to be bad for him to go to the doctor. But, I'll see him in an hour or so when he gets done for our daily routine; a game of checkers. In the meantime, I'll be checking out a few more books.

Fiction, Biographies, they're all the same once you read enough of 'em. But I love sports' articles; man, it just seems like I'm missing so much. Kobe and Shaq broke up the dream team, now the NBA is looking for another dynamic duo. Mc'Run, on the other hand, only goes for Documentaries and Autobiographies. I don't know why, he's old enough to make one of his own.

Just as I select Mildred Taylor's "Road to Memphis" and step off of the shelf, I immediately realize that I'm now surrounded by about five or six Serious 7's. One of them, the one in the center, cracks a smile.

"Going somewhere?"

If I've learned anything in my time here at North Branch Correctional Institute, whatever the situation you never show fear. It can be one guy or 1,000 of them, you never show fear, and you never back down.

"Ah what, you don't speak?"

The other guys start their smirks and giggles; meanwhile I'm still trying to think of a strategy. It's me, the table in front of me, and them. Think fast Cam, think fast.

In the middle of them laughing, I kick the table in front of me, knocking three of them down. I bomb-rush the one on the right with two hard cover books that I have in my hand and duck from the person that I know is coming behind me. He ends up hitting his own man; that's two down. And four more are coming. With no other aids, it's time to throw-down. One of them hits me from behind, and on the floor I go. I didn't stay there long though; someone else comes and appears to be helping me. With someone in my corner, I go back at it. Now standing, I get a clear view of the person standing next to me, Robinson (the same guy who robbed Yang's store, the same guy who watched Sondra be murdered, the same guy responsible for me being in here). I wonder what that's about. But in no mood to argue, I have to take whatever help that I can get. Within minutes, officers arrive, and into the hole we go for another four months.

****

Zay

September 02, 2009

Cold and dark, lonely as ever, I hate the hole even in the best of weather. What did I do? What have I done? Betrayed the set for an army of one. Now I'm dead on either side, but with a sentence like mine's, who cares about the things that I've left behind; leaving behind old friends and horrible memories, only to trade them in for a forgiving symphony. Could I be forgiven for the things that I've done? Hopefully, because my life's redemption has just begun.

I'm fresh out of the hole, with not a friend in sight, because no one wants a trader in their life. Ron, though still my roommate, won't be caught dead with me just to save face. But I don't care, because I did what I knew to be right. It comes a time when you have to make these types of decisions in your life.

Staring at some half cooked eggs and plainly cooked grits, it's no wonder why people lose so much weight in this prison. Just as I move to put a spoonful of unsalted grits into my mouth, I look up to see two people walking over to me, Johnson and his friend Mc'Run. I watch in awe as the two of them sit down with me. The table of one has now become the table of three.

"So what are you up to?" I ask, trying to appear to be cool with the situation at hand.

Giving me one quizzical look, Johnson smiles and says, "Shoot man, trying to eat my breakfast."

We both burst out laughing.

Mc'Run just smiles seemingly glad that the two of us seem to be getting along.

"I'm Cameron, Cameron Johnson. But most people call me Cam," he says, stretching out his hand in a friendly gesture.

"Zaycon Robinson, but you can call me Zay." We shake on it, and from that moment on, he becomes my best friend, sticking closer than a brother.

***

Cam

June 17, 2014

"That's game." I throw down my last card in spades. It's hard to play Sspades with three people, but hey, it can be done. Down time in the mess hall rarely occurs, but when it does, we try our best to enjoy it. With a room full of inmates, you can barely hear yourself think.

"Man, you always be cheating," comments Zay, sarcastically.

"In my opinion, both of ya'll cheat," chuckles Mc'Run as he folds his playing hand.

"Say what you want, but I still won! Who's up for a game of checkers?"

"Nah man, you got it," laughs Zay, all because he lost the past 3 games.

Just as we are about to move on and switch games, in walks Officer Mc'Nair. Everyone stiffens up, preparing themselves for some long lecture. Man, I wonder what's going on now.

"Quiet everyone. Daniel Summit, Roger Taylor, Cameron Johnson, Calvin Hall, Terry Beachton, and Zaycon Robinson. . ." Looking up from the white paper in her hand, she stares at each and every one of us. "There's been some investigation into your cases. Turns out that the prosecutor who tried each of you has been found guilty of tampering with evidence in each of your cases, and therefore, the judge has decided to overturn your convictions. Congratulations gentlemen, you're free to go!"

What! The entire room erupts with sounds of joy. Wow, look at God. . . .

Chapter 5

Zay

August 19, 2014

Back on the streets, roaming through the city, only God has been the one riding with me. No more cells, not even a home, I just don't know where I really belong. I never pondered on the day that I'd finally get to see my brother, but still, it has come clearer than the words 'FREE' typed out on my letter. How did I beat a sentence filled with 'his' time? How was I ever to come back to this life of mine? Now my future is closer than it appears, I can't wait to find out what God has in store for the next couple of years.

"Finally!!" I exclaim, as I lay back on my bed exhausted from the day's events. Taking another glance at my one bedroom apartment, I'm feeling pretty good about myself. It turns out that the government has programs for people just like me, fresh out the joint and eager to get a brand new start. Shoot, I got an apartment, a cellphone, and to top it off, I even got an interview with some construction big-wig somewhere downtown. I guess, Baltimore it is.

Knock! Knock!

Man, I just got here, who could it be? "Who is it?"

"The Police, now open up."

It ain't nobody but Cam, always playing. I get up laughing and open the door anyway.

"Hey man, what's up?"

"Nothing much, I see that you've settled in already."

"Yeah, yeah, I tried to, but hey, we have to start somewhere," I say, looking around my barely furnished apartment.

"Right, right, but 'aye, you want to go down the street and get something to eat."

"Man, I don't know. I was just going to order in."

"Man please, you in my city now."

"Yeah, alright." And we're off. Both of us are laughing and joking as we jet off into the city streets. Getting used to the freeman's air, we trot on.

***

Zay

Present Day

Cam found out that his mother moved away, and that his brother Lamar was given up for adoption. Despite such challenges, Cam went on to become a writer for the sports section in the city's newspaper. Sports were always his thing. And just like he always dreamed, 'He went big' as far as Baltimore is concerned. He ended up getting married, and settling down with a family of his own. Last June, he welcomed a baby boy.

And me, myself, I went on to finish my Associate's degree. Soon after, I became a welder for D&C Inc. When I first got out of prison, I tried to look for Kenny, but as fate would have it, Kenny was found dead in his apartment three Christmas' ago. No suspect has ever been charged.

Knowing Kenny, his bad attitude and obnoxious language probably had something to do with it.

When I fully gave my life to Christ a couple of months ago (with Cam cheering me on from the pews), I stood up in church and told my testimony. And the preacher said something to me that kind of stuck with me. He asked, "Are you what you are because of who you are, or are you who you are because of what you are?" After considering that question for quite some time, I've come to realize that I'm both. I've learned so many lessons in life because of the experiences that I've faced being a product of the streets. Yet, my God-given will to fight for what is right is something that would've blossomed no matter where I was. And yes, it took everything that I've gone through to get me to where I am today; alive and saved. It's my belief that everybody's task in life is to find out who they are, but the things that happen along the way both shape and re-create the individual itself. I've always longed for family and a close friend; who knew that I would've found him in the very store that I robbed. Seeing him go through life with such positivity gave me purpose, it made me believe that all my pain and suffering was worth it. God took my only brother and gave me my closest friend, now we're both men trying to reshape the world that we live in.

Runaway Home

Chapter 1: March 9, 1953

As a child, I often thought that life's fairytale could one day be mine. A loving mother, who not only looked at her children, but in all honesty actually recognized that they were there. A father who would literally spend all day working, providing for his family and when he'd come home, he'd actually have a smile on his face instead of Jack Daniel in his hand. He'd greet his children with love and joy, not with the worn side of his belt. But I guess fairytales are just little stories, life's way of reminding you of everything that somehow ignores you!

I'd spent all day playing. Now, I find myself racing to church. I've got two miles to go and no time to spare. Oh, how did I let it get so late? As I run through the wooded path, a shortcut at best, I'm careful to heist my dress, keeping it free from snags. Oh, momma would sure tear my hid if she knew that I'd skipped school today.

"Come on Linda, you're going to have us late."

"I'm coming just as fast as I know how."

"Well, go faster," yelps Peggy, who happens to be a little ways ahead of me. You see, the woods must've been her home, because she's just a dodging and weaving all out in front of me. While I'm following behind trying to keep pace, but needless to say, my legs aren't as fast these days. Huffing and puffing, I pass by a tree, anxious to take a breath.

"Come on, I'm not getting in trouble 'cause of you," Peggy calls from a distance without stopping a lick. "The sun is going down. Hurry up!"

Reluctantly, I press on, "Ouch!"

"What's wrong?" Peggy stops and turns around, hearing the agony in my voice.

I look down to see what actually has me. "Oh gosh, I'm stuck!"

"In what?"

"I don't know, looks like a thorn bush."

Peggy doubles back, trying desperately to pull me out. I swear, the harder she pulls, the more pain I feel.

"Ouch . . . Hey, watch it!"

"Stop fussing. You're almost out."

With one or two more tugs, I'm finally free. Only to have torn stockings and a now dirty, snagged-up school dress; so much for keeping clean. Again we press on, almost to the roadway now, and then we see it; a gang of cars cruising slowly as if looking for something. So close to the road way, Peggy and I find the nearest shrub and crouch behind it as if to make ourselves invisible. Then suddenly, the vehicles stop. The people that jump out sound like men, but they look like the white-sheeted monsters that my grandma told us about. According to her, they went about the South seeking and searching for any colored child known to be what they called 'trouble.' And she'd tell us, "If you're in the streets long after dark, you're in trouble, and the monster is going to tear your hid." I never thought that I'd see one for myself. I hold Peggy's hand as tight as I can. If that monster was out to get me, he'd have to get us both. I feel on the ground with my free hand to grab some sticks, rocks, or anything else that I could use to fight my way out. In the midst of my thoughts, I can hear her sobs. I turn to her and even in the darkness I can still see the fear in her eyes. I can't believe it. Dare-devil Peggy really *is* scared of something, but sadly, so am I.

Hearing a car door slam, my mind jolts back to reality. Peering to the road, I see them, maybe fifteen or twenty of them, all holding torches, all rambling in chatter. Then a few of them go to the trunk of one of the vehicles and retrieve something. I try squinting my eyes to make the image just a bit clearer. Then it dawns on me, they pulled out a colored man bound in rope. The man appears to be somewhat frightened, but somehow, he looks to be composing himself far better than we are. Did he know what was coming? I know that we didn't. . .

As the monsters come closer, still with the constant chatter, the man's face slowly comes into view. Why, it's Mr. Jimmy, Mrs. Baultman's grandson. Why, he had been educated some time up north. After the passing of his mother, he and his family decided to move back home. He said that he'd seen the world, and now it was time for family. He came down here, opened up his own shop and everything. He calls it 'Sweet Heaven.' It sells all kinds of pies, cakes, candy, and treats. Momma bought six sweet potato pies from him last weekend. Being so close to town, I stop by his shop most days after school to get some Mary Janes and Sugar Babies for just a Nickel. He's about medium height and always well groomed.

I can't think for the life of me why the white-sheeted monsters would get Mr. Jimmy. What kind of trouble was he in? Getting closer, the men stop at an opening just to the right of us. The men stop by an old oak tree and proceed to place a rope around Mr. Jimmy.

With a sigh, Peggy gasps, "They're going to hang him!"

Judging from the looks of things, she's right. 'Cause before we know it, the monsters begin to fasten the rope so tight, that it starts to lift him off of the ground, or so it looks. Mr. Jimmy is so high that he has to stand on his tippy-toes on the stool up under him. Then suddenly, one of the monsters yanks the stool from underneath Mr. Jimmy's feet. With that, the crowd of monsters begin to let out a joyous yell, raising their torches. All the while, Mr. Jimmy is gagging time and time again, as if trying to breathe above water, jerking his feet relentlessly. Then, as if to add to his pain, the white-sheeted monsters take their torches and put them on Mr. Jimmy. And within minutes, though it seems like hours, Mr. Jimmy's feet stops jerking. He stops trying to gasp air, and suddenly, he begins to sway on the rope, back and forth as if he's given up the fight and finally succumbs to fate. Though the right of speech escapes me, warm tears roll down my cheeks. And with that, the white-sheeted monsters return to their cars and drive off one by one, leaving Peggy and I alone with Mr. Jimmy, who's still swaying, still burning.

Looking up at the sky, we are way late for church. But at the moment, it doesn't seem all that important. In more of a shock than a rush, Peggy and I run the rest of the way; not speaking, just holding hands and crying our own private tears. Reaching the church grounds, we stop just short of the door. Oh how the sound of the congregation resonates in our hearts. They are singing, *"Holy Ghost, don't leave me. I need you to guide me on my way."*

As we enter, I see people dancing joyously and praising the Lord, but one look at us and the church goes silent. Peggy and I walk to the altar and stop. My white dress is now covered in dirt, and my stockings are torn this way and that. Peggy's dress appears to be just as unkempt as mine and just as soaking wet as can be. Come to find out, Peggy was so scared, she'd peed on herself, but mixed in with the dirt, you really couldn't tell it. The louder the silence, the more we begin to cry, and this time as frantically as we know how.

I see Peggy's mother rushing toward her, shaking Peggy as if she's about to shake the devil out of her. "Child, what's wrong with you?" Peggy, who is speechless, shakes her head and cries even louder.

"Peggy. . . . Peggy!"

"Linda, what in God's name happened to ya'll? And where have ya'll been?" Momma asks me as if she actually cares. I tell you, if you saw her in front of folks, you would think that she's a fairytale mom for sure. "What's wrong child?"

"Jimmy . . . Mr. Jimmy. . ." Between sobs. "We saw . . . Mr. Jimmy. . . .The white-sheeted monsters. . . .They. ..They . . . ---"

And with that, Mr. Jimmy's wife, who had been rocking their youngest child to sleep, passes the baby to the person sitting next to her and leaps toward us, "Jimmy? My Jimmy? What happened?"

"They. . . They. . ."

"Ahhh... They hung him." It amazes me how Peggy was so distraught to talk when they asked her, but she can finish my sentence right off.

Whatever it was, that was all it took. The entire church begin to feel the reality of the situation. Scanning the crowd, Mr. Jimmy's oldest son, Jr., a classmate of mine (who was often quiet and to himself), stares at me blankly. His eyes were asking questions that my soul didn't have the answer to, so I avoid them wholeheartedly and resort to sheltering my own tears.

Chapter 2: September 5, 1962

Growing up in the wild,
One could become weak.
But that's the very time that
You get to find out just who God made
You to be

    Sitting outside, I let the raw words run through my mind. Man, I haven't been here in years. In the fall of '55, momma finally got the nerve to leave daddy. But however good that was for her, I can't say the same for my brothers and I. Donnie and Frank quit school and went out to the fields to find work. And I, well let's just say that when momma left, instead of serving as dad's punching bag, I took to my school work. Donnie supported me through high school and college too, but in June, everything changed. While working at the railroad, where daddy's been working for about fifteen years, he was going about his daily duties drunker than most. Somehow or another, his foot got stuck on the track, and he just couldn't seem to get free before the next train could come by. So, that's how I ended up back here; someone had to maintain the house. Donnie and Frank each have families of their own to support, so that left me. It's crazy how I spent years of running from this town only to be brought back years later.

    At first, I was keen to the idea of maintaining the only thing that my family has left. But now that I'm here, it just doesn't feel like home, not anymore. With each room holding its own closet of secrets, I spend most of my time outside, vowing to let life's past die on its own. From where I sit in grandpa's rocker, I can spot Peggy's house down the road, the church steeple behind Aunt Elma's and Uncle Red's house, and the Collier farm which looks like a white blanket with all that cotton sprouting out. Shoot, I guess this year's cotton yield is going to better than usual.

"Hey, good looking."

"Hey, Donnie," I reply as he is coming into the yard tired, sweating up a storm.

"What's been keeping you out here?"

"Nothing"

"Shoot, when you were little, we used have to drag you outside. So I know something's up."

"Ha! Ha! Very funny wise guy!"

Reaching the steps, Donnie sits down and gazes into the distance.

I tell you, I don't know how Paula deals with him. With his hat cocked to the side, a toothpick is in his mouth, and torn work pants, he's every bit of the poor and needy, I swear.

"Well, you know a lot's been changing over the last couple of years."

"Yeah, I can see that."

"How so? Seeing as you haven't even left the steps yet?"

"Child hush, I haven't been gone that long and besides there's never been anything to see in Trenton, Mississippi."

"Please! Mr. George has a thrift shop on the corner of First and Lafayette," He states, pointing out each grave improvement to me as if it somehow adds to the town's significance. "The city's brought in two factories which has brought in as many jobs as the stars in the sky! Oh and Peggy's…"

"Ok Donnie, I get it," I say, sounding as irritated as ever.

"Well . . . ok then, be like that. But speaking of Peggy, you happen to run into her yet?"

"Nope, not lately."

"How can you, seeing as how you haven't even left the porch since you've been back."

"Whatever, Donnie!" cutting him off, as I shake my head and roll my eyes at the notion of making this town feel anything like home.

Still staring at me with a mouth so wide that a fly could've flown in it, Donnie gets up, locks the front door and pushes me out of grandpa's chair. Jolted and shocked, I whip around to give Donnie a piece of my mind.

"What was that for?"

"You! Seeing as how all this city living has made you too good to slum with us country folks, huh?"

"What? What are you talking about?"

"Oh, us working folks aren't good enough for you now?"

"What? No."

"Yeah, well I have news for you. It was this working man that worked two jobs, cleaned up lawns, and whatever else that I could to put your uppity self..."

"Hey! That's not fair. Look, I'm sorry that you couldn't seem to make it out of this slop hole, but, that's no fault of mine. I never asked you to do any of those things. All I ever wanted to do was to get out of this place and make a decent living for myself, not to slave in somebody's kitchen and beg for somebody else's seconds. I never wrecked your life. I just found mine. So please, have some decency about yourself and stop taking your frustrations out on me. If you didn't make something of yourself, it's because of you not me. . . .Not me!" Now furiously yelling at the top of my lungs.

Within two shakes, I feel it. The warm leather side of a back hand, a feeling that I know well. It's powerful blow rocks me to my core. With that one motion, my body is lunged from the step to the ground. Feeling the tingle on one cheek, and grass burns on the other, I jump to my feet to face my perpetrator. No longer twelve years old, I refuse to relive my past. With one moment of fight, I lunge at my brother. I never wanted to take it from my father and I'm sure not going to take it now. In a rage, I start to hit Donnie with everything left in me.

"Stop, Linda, this is childish!'"

Trying his best to take control of the situation, he tries to block me and push me off, but it's far too late for that. "Hey . . . . Stop . . . . I'm not playing now. . . Hey... Stop." With one backward push, my back collides with a post on the porch and I tumble to the ground again flat on my face.

"I said stop, you hear."

Sobbing uncontrollably, and in a world of pain, I try to stand, but my body is in no shape to jump back up as quickly. I'm dirty, with blood running down my dress, and as unkempt as ever. Still not willing to give up the fight, I scrap every inch of the ground looking for some kind of help. I tell you the truth, there's nothing on this ground but grass and rocks, but today, they'll have to do. I clump up handfuls at a time and lunge them like grenades in Donnie's direction. Judging by his yells, I can tell that some of them hit the target. Satisfied at the findings, I throw more of them.

"Hey now. . . 'Aye. .. .I already told you to stop," He yells, shielding himself from my blows. "Alright . . . Ok then. ... Just get on out. . . . Get on out of here now."

Now standing, still cradling rocks, I back my way to the fence. "I will. . . And I ain't ever coming back. . .You hear! . . . .I'm never coming back. . . .Never!"

And with that, I slam the fence and run as fast as my legs will take me, this time, not looking back. I can hear Donnie still yelling in the distance, but with every step, I begin to tune him out, one word at a time.

Dazed and confused, I don't know anything else to do but run. I need to get away; I've got to get away. The harder I cry, the faster I run, passing Ella's house (even with her constant calls from the door). I guess even she saw Donnie and I fighting. Huh, figures. Ignoring her, I keep going. I tell you, this is why I hate this neighborhood so much; time something happens, everybody's peeping out of the door. I ran pass the church and it looks like a crowds already gathered. I guess Wednesday night bible studies are still mandatory for most folks. Into the woods. . . Run, run, run . . . After a while, I begin to see the clearing, the dusty paved road which glistens even as the sun goes down. This spot, this very spot which I've managed to avoid for almost ten years is right in front of me. With no words and no thoughts, I run and then, it happens. Hearing a honking horn, I turn into the light of someone's high beams.

"Hey lady, watch out!" The driver courageously tries to swerve, but it's too late. . . . .

****

September 8th

To dream a dream that's nearby yet so far, I'm faced with the task of considering my heart. Broken though it be, to mend it I must; but how can I do such a thing, when there's no one that I can trust. This void in my heart, oh please let it move away from me, so that I can escape this mood. Mood of depression, and years of self-doubt, oh how have I finally come to the place of being without?

"Now Lord, please cover this here child. . ."

Oh how tired am I! As I motion to move my head, the pain in my nerves jolt me back to reality. Man, what happened?

". . . and Lord, we stand here knowing that You can do all things Father. . . ."

Oh God, who is that praying at the top of his lungs? Someone is yelling, shouting, and making all kind of fuss. Doesn't he know that God ain't deaf! Attempting to move yet again, I try my best to move my toes, but I guess they're sleeping too good to move right now.

". . . AND NOW LOOOOOOORD! Open a door dear Lord, that no man. . . .No man can close and pleaaaaasssssssseeeee Loooooooooooord."

Oh Jesus, I tell you if that man don't hush his darn mouth. I already have a headache; what else is he trying to do? Send me to the grave on an early arrival.

". . . .Amen, Amen, and Amen." Amen Lord!

"Thank you Pastor Burke. We really appreciate you coming out like this."

I haven't even opened my eyes yet, but I can tell you from a mile away that that sounds like Donnie. The absolute last person that I have a mind of seeing today. With that note, child, I just lost my desire to move. I don't plan on seeing that Negro on my worst day, which so far, happens to be today.

"Oh, anytime Donnie. Why, you guys are like family to me. I remember ya'll growing up."

Yeah, I remember you too, and judging from seeing you last, nothing has changed. Always with a top hat, suit jackets too tight to fit, still rocking that Christmas wreath haircut, with his pants' legs just begging to reach his ankles. Can somebody please tell this man that high waters are not in style; and if he's going bald, he should stop trying to revive his hair and just cut it off. Lord, bless my soul.

"Yessa"

"Why, you, Frank, and Lin'na grew up like three peas in a pod."

For heaven's sake, can someone please tell that man that my name is L-I-N-D-A, not Lin'na. Oh Lord, sleep, sleep. ... Please find me. So, I tune out the rest of the conversation and postpone my troubles for another day. Sleep. . .Sleep. . . Sleep. . .

***

As I open my eyes for the first time in a few days, with the sun peeping through the window, it takes a minute or two for my eyes to re-adjust. Looking around the room and then at my covers, I immediately recognize this room as being none other than my bedroom. Looking from my hands down to my covered up toes, I notice someone at my side. I nudge him with the few fingers that I have that aren't sleep. The little boy, no more than five or six, raises his head slowly. After wiping his sleepy eyes, he takes a second look. After a minute or two, the boy springs out of his chair, nearly knocking it over, and darts into the next room yelling at the top of his lungs, "Mom. . . .Dad.... She's up. That lady's up!"

I lift my head watching, waiting to see who exactly his folks were, and trying to figure out exactly why he was watching me. Well, I didn't have to wait long. Within seconds, in comes Paula and Donnie along with two other children who hopelessly follow behind.

"Oh my Lord!" exclaims Paula as if she'd just seen a fine car and a brand new house.

"She's awake. Thank you Jesus!" Donnie shouts, smiling from ear to ear.

Though still terribly upset with him, I'm in far too much pain to complain, so I force a smile of recognition.

"Hey good looking, it looks like 'never' came sooner than you thought!" He laughs at his own attempt of making a joke.

Really Donnie?

Chapter 3: November 19, 1962

As I stand at the window and watch the wind blowing the leaves to and fro, I tell you that that's the first real sign of winter cheer.

"Will you stop gazing and start helping?"

I turn and look up at my old friend Peggy. Peggy and I really haven't seen or heard much from each other in years, but she hasn't changed a bit; still bossy. However so, I make my way over to the table. "Help with what? You got it."

"Linda, if you don't pick up a cloth, I know something. The mothers are preparing a meal and it's our job to clean the dining room and decorate it with Thanksgiving colors," She smirks, motioning as if to prove her point.

"Peggy, this is a church. I thought that the cross was decoration enough?"

Annoyed, Peggy walks off chattering to herself about my so called 'laziness.'

Now how am I supposed to decorate with this construction paper (in every color but orange) and ribbons all scattered on the kitchen table? Well, I've got to start somewhere. So, I proceed to pick up the broom. Seeing me doing something of use, Peggy decides to join in. She cleans every table. Thinking back, Peggy and I parted ways after high school. I wanted more, and all she wanted was right here in Trenton. And there I was thinking that we would be together forever. Turns out, she's gotten married and has a child of her own, a baby girl named Zeah. I tell you the truth; it looks like everyone's got someone but me. Anyways, after my accident, she told Donnie and Frank that she would take care of me. That way, they could go back to work and report to their own families. Once my condition improved and I was back to myself, she said that it would be robbery if I didn't give back to the Lord somehow. So here I am, and Pastor Burke couldn't have been happier. According to him, I'm finally following in my mother's footsteps. With no real skills to cook, clean or to make people's lives a living hell, I've resorted to what I do best, teach. I started teaching the youth, along with some adults, (those who either couldn't attend school or dropped out of one) how to read and write on church nights. Now, I've only been teaching for about a week or two, but my class is steady growing.

Ahhh man, tell me this place has a dust pan. Dog-gone-it, well I'll do it the old fashion way and sweep it outside. Makes no nevermind to me. Sweep. . . .Sweep. . . Sweep. . .

"Oh, I'm sorry sir. I didn't see you." Of all the luck, I swept dirt onto a man's foot, and around here, people don't like you sweeping dirt onto their feet. When you do that, someone they love is supposed to die real soon. "I'm so sorry . . ."

Not really knowing what else to do, I take a cloth and try my best to clean it off.

"Oh, you're alright. . . I guess," he says, moving his feet and giggling. "Seeing as how a little dirt ain't ever hurt nobody."

Our eyes dance for a second or two and he walks on. Though not much for grooming, he's rugged as can be. Being a tall, dark man, he reminds me of a cowboy, but a cute one. And as he passes me, he smells every bit of fried chicken. I guess they have him outside cooking.

"Well, I'll be. Aren't you just the charmer?"

I snap back to reality.

"Oh hush Peggy. You're too much for me. All I was doing was apologizing…"

"All you was doing was trying to court you a man."

"Oh please, and if I was, which I'm not, it sure wouldn't be him. I like my men to dress up and look nice for a lady."

"Oh, you like your men to dress up!" She begins to dance around, mocking me as best she can. We both start laughing.

"Child please, I saw you eyeing him."

"No, I wasn't eyeing him; he was eyeing me. Guess he liked what he saw!"

"Girl please. You're only one of the few. That's James Hardaway! But everybody calls him Jr."

"Hardaway, I'm not sure that I know any Hardaways."

"Yes, you do. Remember Mr. Jimmy, the one who owned that sugar shack down by the school and called it 'Sweet Heaven?' That's his oldest boy."

"Wow, I never thought that I'd lay eyes on any of Mr. Jimmy's children seeing as how his wife packed up and moved back to Virginia after his death."

"Well, they are in Virginia, but I guess he's truly his father's son. As soon as he got of age, he packed up and moved back here. He said that family mattered, no matter how far. He's been back about six or seven months now helping his great-grandmother, Mrs. Baultman, get around."

"Mrs. Baultman? That spring chicken! Well at 73, she gets around better than I do." Both of us start laughing. Shoot, Mrs. Baultman mows lawns, plants her garden, tends her chickens, and still has enough energy to whip up dinner. She'll clearly out do me any day.

"Well, whatever the case, He's helping her out. And let Mrs. Baultman tell it, she's finally glad to have a real man helping out around the house."

"You know, now that you've mentioned it, I think I remember Jr. He used to be a quiet mouse in school. You remember?"

"Yeah, but not anymore. He runs women during the day, spends most of his nights at the juke drinking and gambling, and still finds time to make it to church on Sunday mornings."

"He's sure different from his daddy."

"That's for sure."

"Man, I never would've thought about seeing him, and the first time we meet happens to be at church."

"Well really, it's the second." Confused, I turn to look at Peggy questionably.

"Second?"

"Yeah! You don't remember anything do you? Why Jr.'s the one who found you laying on the road back there. He said that when he came by, you were sprawled out on the pavement flat as a pancake. It was him who put you in his car and rushed you to the hospital." Shocked, I stare in the distance trying desperately to brace back my own tears.

"Honey, I don't know what he was doing on that road at that time of night, but whatever it was, you better be glad that he came along when he did."

And with that, Peggy and I continue to clean up and finish the decorations, not really talking. Well, I wasn't talking. Peggy continues to rant on and on about how I'm not much in of the mood for conversation. A few 'uh-huhs' and 'sounds good' are enough to suffice Peggy's conversations.

Thanksgiving dinner is a hit, if I have to say so myself. With a little prayer, good food, and plenty of folks, that's the recipe for anyone to have a good time. After eating, the musician gets on the piano and everyone who can get up and move is dancing. Everyone except for me of course. I just reside to watch and laugh endlessly. Watching all of my friends and family having such a good time makes me wonder, 'how do I get to that pace?' I mean, they just look so happy and content. How do I find my happiness? After being lost in thought for a little while, I now realize that I don't have any more juice in my cup. So, I get up and proceed to the refreshment table to once again make the terrible choice of choosing lemonade over sweet tea. With my cup now full to the brim, I motion to take another sip, and then I see it. Why, it's that Hardaway boy staring me dead in my face from way across the room. Not willing to make this situation any weirder than it already is, I quickly turn away and go back to my seat. As I glance back across the room, he's still looking at me. Realizing that I now know that he's been watching me, he cracks a smile, turns up his drink, and heads out the door. With a crowd of people still dancing and entertaining themselves, I'm forced with the decision of staying here or following him. Knowing that I should stay, I get up anyway, and step out into the cold. I'll only be a minute, or so I thought. And with that, I'm out the door helplessly following a man whom I've had no intentions of getting to know for myself. I simply just want to thank him for saving me that day. I had to thank him.

On the chase of the Hardaway boy, I follow him through the woods, staying as quiet as can be. As I cross the paved road, I look up and the sun is going down. Oh, I hate it out here, but I'm too far to turn around now. So I follow him on and on. Then suddenly, he stops, rests on a stump and stares off into the distance. Unsure of what to do, I stand on the paved road. I know this place all too well. Why, this is the exact place where the white-sheeted monsters hung Mr. Jimmy. Yeah, I remember it alright.

"Well, are you going to stand there all night?" mumbles Jr., in between lighting a cigarette and puffing his life away.

How'd he know that I was here?

"Well?" he asks questionably.

Not really sure what to do, I reluctantly walk toward the stump, eyeing the scorched tree the whole time. As I near him, the unusual smell of chicken mixed with smoke fill my nostrils. He is a fine man if I ever did see one.

"Long ways from home aren't you?"

"Not quite. When I was a little younger, Peggy and I used to be out this way all the time."

"Why? Was it too boring in town?"

"Actually quite the opposite. You see going through the woods is the quickest way to get to the matinee. Peggy and I used to skip school just to go. During the day, security wasn't as bad, so that was the only time that we could sit in the front seats and not the balcony."

"Bet ya'll would've been in some kind of trouble had ya'll got caught."

"We would've, but the janitor knew my family. And he was too kind hearted to turn us away. So, he told us not to let him see us, because if he did, we'd be in trouble. It was the one day where it wasn't no white/colored only. It just felt good, like the world should be you know." Now standing directly behind him, both of us gaze at the old tree.

"Sounds nice enough. Do you want to sit down?"

"And here I was thinking that the gentleman in you was dead."

Even in the darkness, I can still see his treasured smile, just as handsome as the noonday. He chuckles a little before getting up to offer me the stump. "My lady?"

Oh he is too much for me. I burst out laughing as awkward as ever.

"Ok," I reply, soon realizing that sitting on the stomp isn't as comforting as he'd made it look.

"So tell me, how'd an uppity girl like yourself end up here with us?"

"I didn't go that far?"

"What? Alabama isn't far enough for you?"

"Wow, nothing escapes you does it?"

"No, not really."

"To answer your question, yes I went to Tuskegee and . . . . .Well, my father died and now I'm back, simple as that."

"Simple as that, huh?"

"Yeah, anyway enough about me. What about you?"

"What's to know?"

"From what I hear, apparently a lot, seeing as how this is the second time that I've seen you out here and all."

Highly disturbed, within an instant, James Hardaway straightens his stance, puts out his cigarette, and smirks, "Yeah, well some things just aren't worth telling." And with that, he darts off into another direction, going even further into the woods. With night already here, I personally am not willing to stay here by myself, so again, I pursue him.

"Hey. . . .Hey, where are you going?"

"Come and see."

And so, I follow him again. Within ten or fifteen minutes, I hear the rumpled music, the drunken chatter, and see the dim lights. That shack, if any, is a juke alright. You see, I've heard of this one in particular, but I never knew exactly where it was. Now, I do. Realizing the nature of my surroundings, I stop dead in my tracks. I begin to press my woolen shirt and tightly pent hair. Yep, it's clear that I'm highly overdressed for the occasion.

Looking dead into my eyes, as if he could read my very thoughts, he asks, "What's wrong? Haven't you ever been to a club before?"

I quickly turn away, too embarrassed to say that I haven't.

Feeling as if he had the upper hand, he nears me. He puts his arm around my back and pulls me close as space would allow. Then looking dead into my eyes, he says, "It's not like anything in here is going to hurt you. You know that, right?" Feeling as if I'm unconvinced, he decides to go with the voice of reason. "It seems to me like you have a choice to make. Stay out here and freeze or you can come inside with me, warm yourself, and have some fun."

"Is it safe?"

"Ha! Every where's safe with me."

And that was that. I'm not really sure if it was pity or his Hardaway charm that moved me that night, but whatever the case, I should've said no . . . . But, we live and we learn.

Chapter 4: May 12, 1963

"And that's all I have for you tonight. I'll see you all on Saturday, 6 o'clock sharp. Class dismissed."

Though it's been a long time coming, I must say that I'm extremely satisfied with the nightly turn out. For a little over six months, I've been teaching three nights a week. My class has gone from five members to twenty-five members in just these past few months. I've had to ask Peggy to teach the younger children just so that I can have the freedom to expand the adult class. Even so, Donnie and Frank still haven't found the time to make it out. And needless to say, they're the ones that probably need it the most.

"Well, well I guess it's true. You really can teach an old dog new tricks," jokes Harvey, the local Mr. Fix-It.

He's about a good ten or so years older than I am. But even in his mid-thirties, he's still a great catch: recently widowed, with no kids, makes a comfortable living, and has a decent sense of humor.

"Yeah, I guess you're right."

"You know I never would've imagined that I would have such a good time, but I am."

"I'm glad to hear it," I say, with my sly, flirtatious smile.

"You know, if you're not doing anything later, I'd be glad to walk you home."

With his sparkling brown eyes and gentleman like gesture, I sure would've said 'yes' had Jr. not knocked on the door in his normal Hardaway style.

"Hope I'm not interrupting anything." Even though he knows that totally is.

"Oh no, not at all." I reply as startled as ever.

"Well, maybe I should be on my way. You know I've got an early start in the morning, so I'll see you on Saturday," states Harvey as he grabs his book and heads to the door. Before leaving, he gazes back at me and says, "Maybe some other time, Ms. Linda?"

"Yeah, maybe."

And with that he's gone.

"What's that supposed to mean?"

You know Jr.'s always known for breaking up the perfect moment. Annoyed, I move to finish cleaning off my desk, a sign for him to go about his business.

"Nice seeing you too. What's it been, like four, maybe five days?"

"Ahhh, don't act like that."

"Act like what? Like what you're doing is ok? You know, I heard through the Grapevine that the girl that you were with the other night is married!"

"The great ones usually are."

"Yea, so good luck with that one."

"Humph. . ."

"What's that supposed to mean?"

"Oh nothing. It's cute."

"What?"

"This love-hate relationship that you have for me. You know where you act like you hate me. When really, what you mean to say is. . . ." Clearing his throat, "'Jr. I love you Jr.'"

We both start laughing. I promise you, no matter how mad I am at him; he always knows just what to do to make me laugh.

"Oh, hush."

"I'm just saying, if you want my opinion, I would certainly be ok with that."

"Ha! Ha! I'm sure you are. But how about telling me why you're here?"

"Oh, so now I need a reason to see you?"

"Yeah . . . you do! Class is already over and it's far too early for you to turn in, so what's up?"

"There's this new spot that I heard about a few towns over. How about you come check it out with me?"

"Mmm, go with you? Uhhhh. . .NO!"

"Ah, come on. Why not?"

"Well for starters, it's a school night. You know something that us normal folks live for."

"Ah, come on, you have to come. What's one night? I'll have you back in no time," He says, now face to face with me.

"No, but you can walk me home. How's that?"

"Oh, I see how you do. Today me, tomorrow Harvey."

"Well . . . That's entirely up to you. I mean, I do want to be safe and all, so if you're up for it?"

"Ha! You know you're always safe with me."

****

I feel like I'm walking amongst the living, but yet carrying my casket with me. How can I ever kill the stormy silence within me? A smile on my face with a wound in my heart. Is there any other way out? Of this emotional maze in the dark?

As we lock up and head out, I stand by the church step waiting for Jr. to double check the back door. Looking at my watch, I realize it's a quarter past ten, gee-wheeze. Peggy must've dismissed her class a little early. Caught up in my own thoughts, I barely notice the beaming lights ahead of me.

"Hey, where are you headed?"

I look around in the darkness, and think to myself these two gentlemen can't be talking to me. But not willing to be rude, I muster up the strength to speak anyway.

"A good ways to nowhere."

Oh good, Jr., now beside me, utters a response. Good move Jr., good move.

"Yeah well, maybe ya'll should come with us."

"Where to?" Now, Jr's all bent over near the window of the car as if to close me out of the conversation.

"The old house on the hill. Gerald's trying to rally up as many people as he can for support." Jr looks around suspiciously before continuing to talk, a little quieter than normal. I turn my ear in an attempt to hear anyways.

"Man, they did it again. If we're going to fight it, now's as good a time as any."

"Can it wait a few minutes? I promised the young lady that I'd walk her home." He motions toward me, or as he said it, 'the young lady.'

If he thinks for one second that he's about to dump me off, he's got another thing coming.

"Ain't no waiting. We've got to go now. Now's the time." He turns to me as if to signal to me, it's my cue to leave.

"Well, you heard him," I say, shocking both him and the guy in the window. And with that I proceed to get into the car.

Grabbing me by my arm, as if to have a conscious, Jr. stops me. "No, I can't let you go. This here ain't a place for a lady. Nope, you're going home."

"Ah, Jr. stop jiving. We don't have time for that," shrieks the guy in the front.

Finally giving in, Jr. gets in and we're off. It must've took a long while. So long in fact, that I must've fallen asleep, because by the time we stopped, I had to raise my head off of Jr's shoulder. Gosh, it must be really late by now. What time is it?

Getting out, all I can see are cars, open space, and a little shack to justify the least. Coming closer, I now realize why Jr. probably didn't want me to come; no one is out here but men. As we walk a little closer, I can faintly see a few of them as they look me up and down like I'm the last girl on the slave ship. I pull Jr. close, as if to say 'Sorry boys'.

"I told you that you shouldn't be here."

"Any place you can be, I can too."

"No, you can't. Just listen and don't say anything. You hear me? Nothing."

We settle towards the back of the room, if you can call it any space at all. Only two men were sitting, while the rest of us stood. After a few minutes, the tall, bald man that was sitting, gets up, and proceeds to start the meeting.

"Alright, alright. I'm glad that so many of you made it out tonight, especially under the circumstances. I know it's late, and a lot of you have families to tend to, so I'm going to keep it short. As you all know, I'm a part of the resistance up there in Knoxville. My people have been doing all we can up there demanding our right to be free men. And it's been working as best as the good Lord allows. A few days ago however, we joined with those marching up there in Alabama. And I tell you, Alabama is nothing like Tennessee, or any other state for that matter. They spit fire down there, and mean it to. The devil's got a hold of some souls with this here Jim Crow."

"Yeah, so what do you expect us to do about it?" mutters some man over in the right corner. "We don't want to cause any trouble. We live here, you don't."

The crowd erupts in unanimous agreement.

"Now wait . . . Wait. I know that, but don't you want to do something. Aren't you tired of cowering in front of your children, crying 'Yes sir'? Don't you want to be men again? This is your right, but they're not going to give it to you. No, you're going to have to take it. Take back what's yours, what's mine, and what's ours!" Sensing that he's won the crowd again, the tall bald man continues. "Anyway, about two days ago, the KKK, for what we know, set fire to a local church. That was God's house, and it proves to everyone, yet again, that the white devil has no bounds. The church burned to the ground with three girls inside. Those could've of been my kids, your kids, or even your neighbors children. I know that we are in Mississippi, but from what I know, Mississippi is no better than Alabama when it comes to Jim Crow. We've got to do something. We have to stand up and say, 'Enough is enough.'"

"And how are we going to do that?" cried out someone in the crowd.

"By sticking the white devil where it hurts, their money and their mind. We're going to keep going until we find out what works. If we have to, we'll burn every white owned shop or house in sight until they begin to feel what we feel. We'll make our own Klan, the BPK. . .The Black Pride Klan."

The crowd erupts in support. It breaks my heart to see such savages among us.

"Really? Is that what you plan on doing?"

Silence fills the room. God, I actually said that out loud. Jr. nudges me to hush, but I'm in too deep to turn around now. "My, my, and I thought that I was in the presence of a gentleman. You stand for something alright. You stand for vandalizing people's homes, their livelihood, and the businesses that they worked to build from the ground up. I hate Jim Crow just as much as you do, but I'm not about to sell my soul for it."

The tall man parts the crowd, and walks my way. "So what do you suppose that we do my sister? Stand around and do nothing, and watch helplessly as the white devil--…"

"The devil can take any form, white and black alike. While trying to stop such an obvious problem, let's make sure that the white devil doesn't turn into a black one. As long as we continue to ignore this, things will not change, they'll get worse. I've lived in Mississippi all of my life, and I went to college in Alabama. I've heard about Dr. King, Reverend James, and so many others fighting the good fight in faith."

"And where has that gotten them?"

"Further than you'll ever be. We don't have a skin problem; we have a sin problem. Since we fight not against flesh and blood, we'll need God on our side, don't you think?"

"Oh, a church woman I see."

"So, what do you suggest? That we fight with our fists, terrorize people by night, and be cowards before them during the day. All you will be doing is proving to them what they already know to be true."

"Young lady, the best way is to show them all that we're still strong. I've heard of great leaders myself. The great Malcolm X said himself that if we're afflicted, it's our natural right to retaliate."

"The strength of any man should not be judged by the content of his anger, but in the content of his character. There are other ways, but you must first change to find them. If you see yourself as a weak man, you'll behave like one. Now I may just be a naive young lady, but I know that help is everywhere, you just have to know where to look. We are only caged in our minds, always fighting an unseen battle. If you want to get out, you have to THINK your way out."

"Well, little Ms. Poppy has all of the answers tonight..."

"Wait Tim, the young lady might actually have a point. If we go off and do something crazy, they'll kill us dead just as sure as we're breathing. But. . ." Now getting up from his chair and coming into view, He continues. "If we could get a well-organized strategy, we won't be violating any laws, yet we'll still be getting our point across. You see Tim, we're out of towners, and they'll be looking for us to cause trouble for sure. But a farmer, let's say a share cropper who's lived here all of his life, it'll be much more effective, don't you think? Then it's settled, we'll organize boycotts, sit-ins..."

"And how are we going to get that kind of support? We barely have the support of the town as is."

Feeling as if it's my time to pitch in again, I say, "Why the church of course! It's like I said Mr. Tim, we're going to need God on our side. Don't you think? We'll hold educational briefings and use our connections to arrange events. After all, an educated man is an unstoppable one. We'll stay up to date on events globally whether it be riots, small victories, and even new laws."

"Laws? Ha! Don't you know that there are no laws to benefit us?"

I tell you, this Tim guy means to make a mockery of me.

"Yes laws. Are you familiar with rulings such as Brown vs. the Board of Education, guaranteeing the right of desegregated schools? But you know why we haven't heard of it? Because states like ours are arguing quite realistically that our children are not competent enough to academically survive in a desegregated school. So I say, we start here. We push to break barriers in education, in business, and finally in our society."

"It'll be easier to keep the law rather than break it," says Jr.

Wow, he's finally on my side. I thought that I had lost him there for a minute.

Looking around the room for opposition, but seeing none, Tim finally decides to give in. "Alright, we'll try it your way for a few weeks. We'll take baby steps at first until we note whether or not we've actually made an impact. But if this plan fails, and indeed it will, we'll go back to my plan." As he turns back toward the center of the room, plans for boycotts, sit-ins, and so on start coming from everywhere. This truly is the most alive that I've felt in years.

Chapter 5: July 10, 1963

"Girl what are you gazing for?"

Startled back to reality, yet again, I turn to look at Peggy.

"Girl, I'm just so tired."

"Yeah, I bet."

Looking around the room, it's evident that the room isn't going to clean itself. So, I too pick up a broom and begin to clean the floor. "Girl, I'm serious. And every time I turn around, I promise you these classes are getting longer and longer."

"That's because the classes are getting bigger. And the last time I checked, it was you who choose to tutor three children in between classes."

Boy Peggy just has all the answers tonight, doesn't she?

"I just see something in them. It's a crime and a shame that their parents are contemplating on having them drop out. They could really be brilliant, and that's just what this world needs if you ask me."

"But ain't nobody asking you. And besides, you're not fooling anybody?"

"What are you talking about now?"

"Girl please, I'm married. So don't even act like I don't know what's going on between you and Mr. Hardaway."

"Jr? Girl please!"

"I've been noticing how he's been bringing you lunch every other day, and not to mention how he's become a regular attendant at bible Study. That boy ain't playing; he's here seven o'clock on the dot."

"He just enjoys Pastor Burke's informative lectures on politics and current events. Don't even act like it's me? Girl, a lot of people have been coming to church on a regular basis now, seeing as how Pastor Burke is finally talking about something that matters, other than saving souls."

"Yeah, that was a good idea if I have to say so myself. Those shut-ins and prayer meetings have really encouraged a lot of people. Hey, it even touched Mr. Simms's heart over at *Rosco's Chic & Grill*. Didn't you hear? It took a time or two, but he finally had his servants serve Mr. Louise."

"Yeah I heard. Seeing as how she's practically raised the whole town, even him, he couldn't stand the idea of seeing her beaten or jailed."

"And shoot, I'm actually looking forward to our march to Birmingham. I've been looking for a reason to get these thighs in shape."

"Girl, please!"

"Good Lord!"

"What?"

"Speak of the devil; here he comes now with that brown bag."

I follow Peggy to the window, and sure thing there's Jr. walking up the church yard just as cool as he knows how.

"Girl, I know he means well, but please tell him that lunch has been over. It's time for him to do something new."

"Ha! Ha! Girl, you're a mess!"

Almost exactly on cue, Jr. opens the door finding both of us laughing at each other.

"All man, what'd I miss?"

"A watch obviously. Boy, it's half past eight, lunch has been over."

"Ah, Peggy, go home and aggravate somebody else for a change."

"You don't have to tell me twice." Gathering her things, she says, "I'll see you guys tomorrow."

"Alright, bye girl," I say.

Waiting until every sign of Peggy is gone; Jr. turns to me and says, "Man, she's nosey."

"As always. You got something for me?"

Opening the bag, he pulls out a box. "It's from Tim."

I open it, and read the message inside.

Not waiting for me to finish, Jr. blurts out, "What's it say?"

"The Cocks are refusing to let Maggie enter into Wilson Elementary this fall. Saying that in light of recent threats and him being fired from his job, the father's not prepared to put his little girl in danger as well. Man, we've been studying endlessly trying to prepare her. What a waste!"

"What about the others?'

"Both are smart, but not mentally ready to take on the task."

"But I thought that things were going well."

"It is, but not according to big shot Tim. He's motioning to shut down the entire operation and launch his 'grand plan.'" Jr, obviously furious, paces the floor none stop.

"Is everything alright?"

I look up at Donnie, who must have just walked in.

"Oh Jesus, Donnie you scared me!"

He apparently scared Jr. too, because Jr. stops dead in his tracks.

I get up trying to gather my thoughts. "Well umm, what brings you by? It's pretty late."

Still trying to feel out the situation, Donnie questionably looks from Jr. to me.

"Well, you know between me working and you teaching, we haven't been seeing too much of each other, so I decided to just drop by and walk you home."

"Oh yeah, well you don't have…"

"Hey champ, you don't mind if I take her off of your hands do you?" he asks, in his man of the house voice, looking Jr. dead in the eyes.

Lord, if eyes could kill. . .

"Oh, no, not at all. We were just about to close up shop anyway."

Really, Jr.?

"Well, then it's settled. Ladies first." He gestures for me to lead the way.

After locking up, we proceed to walk home. So far in my thoughts, Lord I forgot that Donnie was even with me. We need something big to happen; something to propel this town forward, something to bring us together. I read once were the people of Montgomery did a bus boycott that rocked the city. With this town's history, nothing like that will even stand a chance.

"I don't like you hanging with that boy so much."

"Well, it's not your decision to make."

"I don't like you with him. Anyway, what's a girl like you hanging with a guy like him so much for anyway?"

"First of all, you need to stop while you're ahead, because you don't even know what you're talking about."

"I know enough. I know that he's been walking you home, keeping you out all time of night, and to say the least, I've never known him to be so involved in church before."

"I thought that would be a good thing."

"You know what I mean. Men like him only come around when they want something. And once they get it, they're on the run."

"Oh God, are you really trying to have this conversation right now? And where are you getting your information from? Harvey? You're not fooling anyone. Frank's been telling me how Harvey's been dropping by the house every so often."

"Harvey's been by trying to catch you. Now there's a decent man. When he wants you, he comes right out and asks, makes it known."

"Ask who? You? You're not my daddy."

"Well, no, but I'm close enough. And besides, somebody has to look after you."

"I'm no child."

"Could have fooled me! You know Harvey, he's been doing real well for himself. He's got a house, a car, a decent job, and he can guarantee you a life far better than the one you're living. Can Jr. offer you anything close to that?"

"Leave him out of it."

"I can't. I've been hearing about how he's been showing up every other day, bringing you lunch and what not."

"Nobody told you that but Peggy."

"Yeah, she did, but she didn't have to, because everybody knows."

Finally reaching the house, I gladly head to my room. I'm so through with him.

"You want something to eat? Paula made chicken and rice."

"No, I'm good. I'm tired. I'm going to bed. Night, Paula."

"Goodnight."

***

After working a full days' work, my body sure is tired; bed never felt so good. But it does no good for me sleeping, because my thoughts are beyond rest right now. And to add fuel to the fire, Donnie was a mess and a half tonight, talking to me like I'm some child or something. He must've lost his mind.

Tap! Tap!

What in the world is that? I know it's not raining.

Tap! Tap!

Lord, look who's at my window in the middle of the night. He's lucky I'm still up. I feel on the dresser for my watch, before stumbling to the window. Gee it's a quarter to twelve. What does he want? Reluctantly, I still open the window. I know it's late, but I still have to hear him out.

"Hey, what took you so long? You sleep?"

"Nah, I'm just keeping the midnight oil. Boy please, what do you want now?"

"Ah, you know me. I'm not much for sleeping. I was just passing through, but hey, come walk with me."

"At this time of night? Boy, you must've lost your mind."

"Nah, not yet. But come on, I'll have you back, I promise."

"Give me a second."

"Alright." And with that, we were off.

I guess Donnie was right about something, 'a girl like me has no business whatsoever hanging with a guy like this,' but its Hardaway, and that's enough reason for me. It didn't take long for us to walk down the road. After all, his grandma's house isn't but a skip and a hop away from mine.

"Come on, follow me."

"Why aren't we going through the front door?"

"What? Please, my grandmother would beat the black off of me coming in this time of night."

Well, he was right about that. Mrs. Baultman's the last person for anyone to play with, and I know one thing for sure, I don't want to be on her bad side. I can't help but laugh at the thought of it.

"I thought you were grown?"

"Not in this lifetime. Now, come on."

Careful not to step on anything, I follow him to the back. Mrs. Baultman may be old, but she can hear a pin drop from a mile away. Just as we get into the room, here comes the floor pats. Oh crap! If she sees me here, the whole towns going to know by tomorrow! Oh Lord, where do I go? Jr.'s in no position to help me. He's too busy changing into his pajamas like he's never left the house. My first thought is to go back out of the window, but it's too late for that, so with one quick movement, under the bed I go. And then, the door opens. Yes, just in the nick of time.

"Jr! Jr!"

"Yes ma'am?"

"Boy, what are you doing?"

"Ma'am?"

"Boy you heard me. Don't make me repeat myself."

"Oh, no ma'am. I was just stretching. I just can't sleep for some reason you know."

"Can't sleep my butt. Boy, you're a lie and the truth ain't in you. Does it look like I was born yesterday?"

"No ma'am."

"Well, you better act like it. Shoot, you had me thinking that somebody was breaking in. And you better not be trying to sneak one of those fast tail girls in here like this is some kind of motel or something."

"A what? No ma'am, that's . . . that's crazy. I would never…"

"Boy, stop lying. Just as sure as the shirt's on your back, you'll do it in a heartbeat. But I've already told you, the only person coming in here is Jesus. Now get back in that bed and act like you've got some sense."

"Yes ma'am."

And with that she's off. We both wait silently until the heavy pats were back where they belonged. Hearing the door close, I gasp and emerge from the hideout. That was a close one. "Smooth, real smooth."

"Ah, hush."

"Boy don't scare me like that no more."

"Keep your voice down, you know she's got bionic hearing."

Still catching my breath, I join him on the bed.

"Do you believe in fate?" he says, half looking at me, more like making a statement rather than a question.

Donnie said that Jr. wanted more from me, and tonight I actually hoped that he had. But no, wrong again. He actually wants to talk, just talk. Darn the luck.

"It depends." Geez, I really hope that this isn't one of those long drown out thoughtful conversations to which I actually have to respond, because today, I'm all out of advice.

"Man when I was little, my dad used to go to the store on nights just like this. He used to say with everybody sleeping, these were his working hours, and sometimes, he'd take me with him. I loved it, because while he was doing paperwork, he'd open the ice cream bar and let me get any kind of ice cream that I wanted."

"Wow that must've been awesome."

"Yeah, it was."

"Hey, do you remember how Peggy and I used to rush over to the shop just as soon as school let out? Man those pocket sized Yandle pies were the bomb."

"Yeah, but you know what was the problem with that right?"

"What?"

"Ya'll ain't never have no money."

Both of us burst into a muffled laughter.

"But that's alright though. Mr. Jimmy took care of us. He would still jam our pockets full with Mary Janes, and then he'd say his favorite line, 'that'll be a nickel Ms. Ma'am.'"

"Yeah, but it's so crazy though. My dad was always doing stuff like that knowing darn well that his pockets couldn't afford it."

"Yeah, he was something. There'll never be another one like him."

"That's for sure. I remember this one time, on a night just like this one, he and I went to the store just like always. He'd settled into his work and I'd long since fixed me a birthday cake cone when she came to the door. I'll never forget it. It was raining that night, but she didn't have on any shoes, her hair was all messed up, face was all bloody, and both her blouse and her skirt (if that's what you'd call it) were ripped half off her body. Dad always locked the door at nights, but she didn't care. She kept beating on the door saying 'Help me, help me.' She did it in such a way that even I got scared. And then this dude came up, but I could never see his face. The only thing that I saw were his boots. It was so crazy to me how the color of the brown boots that he had on matched her skin color. Before I could see anything else, my dad ran to the door, and told me to hide behind the counter. When my dad got outside, he stepped in front of the girl with the only weapon that he had in the store, a bat, but he wasn't scared. I could remember being so proud of him and scared for him at the same time. The guy stopped right in front of my dad and said, 'Boy, this ain't your problem. Now you best be going.' But my dad didn't move. He told the man that we didn't want any trouble and to just leave the girl alone. But the man, obviously drunk, jumped on my dad. And daddy, he didn't do anything. He didn't even try to fight back. When I saw him hit the ground, I ran outside to help him. Being no more than eleven or twelve myself, I can remember trying to pull this guy off of daddy. I pulled so hard that his shirt ripped. Daddy kept yelling, 'No, no Jr.' But it was too late, the man knocked me down, and before I could move, he had his hands around my neck. And for the first time, I saw his face; he was a white man. The girl tried to stop him; she jumped on his back, but like a wild horse, he threw her off. Man, I thought that I was gone for sure. But daddy came behind him, and hit the back of his head like a baseball on the run. After a few more licks, daddy couldn't do it anymore. Seeing the man crawling on his knees, hurled over in pain must've hurt daddy to his heart, because daddy put the bat down and told the man not to come around there anymore. The man left, still breathing threats. But I didn't care, I was so proud of daddy because he actually had the courage to fight. When we came back in the store, like a fool, I was so busy telling daddy how good he did, replaying the fight line by line, that I didn't even see the tears running down his face. In the middle of me talking, daddy pulled me close, holding me with both of his hands. He made me swear not to tell anyone, not one soul, what had happened. He kept saying, 'You were never here. You hear me? You were never here.' Then he hugged me, not like a regular hug, but he held me tight, like he was never going to let me go. And he kept saying, 'I love you. I'm so sorry,' over and over again. I was so young that I didn't fully understand what he meant by that. Two days later, my dad was gone, dead, hanging from a tree like some criminal. I couldn't even go to his funeral, because I kept feeling as if it was my fault somehow. And all I want to do, so bad, is to just tell him how sorry I am."

It pains my heart seeing a man cry, but I knew Jr.'s story all too well. For years, I've been wondering what Mr. Jimmy did that was so wrong. Now I know, he was found guilty of defending his son. As I reflect on the horrors of that night, hot tears sting my face. Help us Lord. Unable to comfort Jr., I embrace him as much as I can. For with years of wasted grief, that's all that I have left in me.

He pulls himself together, "Man, I really didn't mean to cry all over you like that. This is so not how I had this evening planned out."

Staring at him eye to eye, "Well how was it supposed to be?"

And with that, he gently pulls me close, and kisses me. Not like a thank you kiss, or a glad to know you kiss, but a real, hold-up-wait-a-minute-shut-the-front-door-and-bring-me-the-bacon type of kiss. With my mind telling me to stay and my heart telling me to leave, I have to stop this.

I quickly hit him with the under slide and make my way across the room.

"What's wrong?"

"Everything."

"Which part?"

"Look, I'm sorry. I thought that this was what I wanted, but... I don't."

"Oh ok. Let me guess, you want Harvey."

"What? No, why does everyone keep saying that?"

"Linda come on, everybody knows that Harvey's been coming around your house night and day like that's his second home."

"It's not that."

"Then what is it?"

"This! So what let me guess, you're going to seduce me, make me fall at your command so that I'll go along with you and Tim on this crazy crusade."

"Now, I'm really confused."

"I found this!" I snap, pulling the paper from my skirt pocket. "Tonight, when Donnie came, you were in such a hurry to leave that you dropped this."

He takes the letter as if it's his first time reading it.

"Oh so what, now you got amnesia? Give it here, let me read it: *'James, after certain findings, the Cocks situation has been resolved. We can now move forward with tentative measures.'* Really? So you had the man fired?"

"No, I didn't. That wasn't me."

"Then who was it?"

"Look, when I came home a few months ago, I had one thing on my mind, and that was to bring my father some justice. I put pressure on the officials and even the courts, but no one was willing to reopen a case in which every big wig in town was a part of. It's like my whole life, people been telling me to leave it alone and just let it go. Well, I can't let it go. I'm a man Linda, and someday when I have a family, I want the right to be one. If no one was willing to help me, I had to find somebody who would."

"Tim?"

"I meet Tim, back home in Virginia. We got into a few tussles along the way, he helped me, and I helped him. He's an old friend who's just as feed up with this as I am. Yeah ok, he may be a little extravagant, but he's not entirely wrong. Why is it so wrong to stand up for yourself? Why is it so wrong to demand to be heard?"

"Because you're not trying to be heard, you're trying to get revenge."

"And what's wrong with that?"

"That's exactly my point. Even now you don't get it, and Tim is not your friend. He's an awful person who thinks about nobody but himself. You're so much better than he is. I just want to know one thing, why did you guys stop the Cock's girl from enlisting in school? That could've given her opportunities and opened doors for the community that we've never even dreamed of. Why? Just tell me that, why?"

"It's because of you. You have this whole philosophy that bringing folks together will make everything ok. You act like nothing's happened, and as long as we can sweep stuff under the rug of forgiveness, everything's alright. Well it's not alright! There needs to be some line at some point that says hey, 'Enough is enough.'"

"You're starting to sound just like him. Is this even about the community anymore? Or is it just about you? . .You know, I've been doing my research as well. And it turns out, Tim and his clan are maniacs. They terrorize their own people just for the sake of doing it. There was no church burning in Cannington. Here's a man who says that he wants peace, yet he's wanted in two states for embezzlement, drug trafficking, and robbery. He cons people and communities out of both time and money. They buy into his big ideas, and in return, he destroys the things right in front of them. As in his BPK crusade, he vandalizes businesses and robs them blind, claiming that they had it coming. He's insensitive and reckless. He doesn't care about anybody but himself. James, I know that you want answers. I know that you want peace, but come on, you can't possibly be thinking about destroying a whole town, your town, because of one man's mistake."

"Are you calling what happened to my father a mistake?"

"No, I'm calling your method of revenge a mistake. Nothing you do is going to bring him back. You can wipe out every business, every neighborhood, and every trace that this town even existed, but that won't change anything."

"I don't want to wipe out anything?"

"Then what do you want?"

Thoroughly frustrated, Jr. collapses on the bed.

"I'll tell you what you want. You want everyone to pay for a terrible, terrible tragedy. I'm not sure whether you want to find him or to find yourself? But I'll tell you something, you better quit while you're ahead. You can't manage yourself as long as you're out there looking for broken pieces." Bending closer to him, I continue, "You've got to move on. Your father died for you. Don't die with him. You've spent your whole life running from yourself: running from regret, running from pain, and from even old memories. And trust me, that's nothing to be ashamed of. We are all running from something at some point in time. You just need to accept what happened and know that there's nothing that you could've done to change it. You were a child! And no, your pain doesn't give you the right to play judge and jury over anyone. If you really want to honor your father, stop slumming through life in a drunken mess, pick up the pieces and be the man that he raised you to be. Trust God and believe that everything is going to be alright."

"I hope you're right about that."

Chapter 6

Marriage is fun,

And life is bliss.

I finally got my

True love wish.

    Well, I guess my talking got through to Jr., because he finally began to do something with his life. For starters, he married me. He re-opened 'Sweet Heaven' right where his daddy used to have it, and he quit his affiliation with the BPK mob, at the right time too. Tim went ahead and vandalized three stores right here on the town's square, but he didn't get far. He got caught two towns over trying to sell the merchandise for some quick cash. Maggie Cocks did go to Wilson Elementary. Despite many struggles, she still managed to make 'A' honor roll. Her parents are so proud of her, and I am too.

    Donnie's always saying something about me being a runaway. He says that I've spent so much of my life running away from my past just to get pulled right back where I started. I think maybe he's right for a change. I've spent so much time running, that I never really knew that everything that I wanted was right here all along. I guess it's safe to say then that I finally have my happiness . . . I've finally found my home.

Other Books By Tatiana Whigham

Do You Know Your Worth?

From Butterflies to Caterpillars

www.ingramcontent.com/pod-product-compliance
Lightning Source LLC
Chambersburg PA
CBHW052051070526
44584CB00017B/2126